THE HISTORY OF GREEK PHILOSOPHY
Volume One: The Pre-Socratics

The HISTORY of

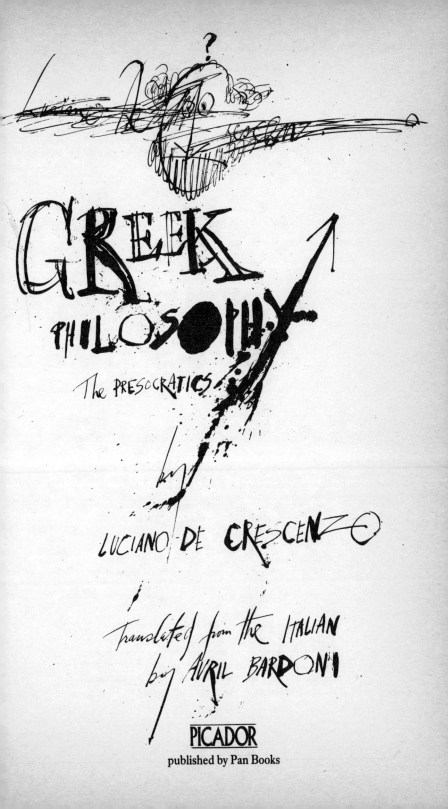

Also by Luciano De Crescenzo
in Picador

Thus Spake Bellavista

First published 1983 by Arnoldo Mondadori Editore S.p.A., Milano
This Picador edition published 1989 by Pan Books Ltd,
Cavaye Place, London SW10 9PG

9 8 7 6 5 4 3 2 1

© Arnoldo Mondadori Editore S.p.A. 1983
Translation © Pan Books Ltd 1989
Illustrations © Ralph Steadman 1989

ISBN 0 330 30485 5

Photoset by Parker Typesetting Service, Leicester
Printed and bound in Great Britain by
Billings and Sons Ltd, Worcester

I write these things as they appear true to me,
because, as I see it, the tales told by the
Greeks are many and humorous.

HECATAEUS, fr.1

Text Illuminations
by
Ralph STEADman

Acknowledgements

The publishers would like to thank the following for permission to use copyright material in this book:

The President and Fellows of Harvard College for extracts from Diogenes Laertius, *Lives of Eminent Philosophers*, translated by R. D. Hicks (Harvard, 1925);

The estate of Aubrey de Sélincourt and Penguin Books Ltd for extracts from Herodotus, *The Histories*, (London, 1954);

J. M. Dent & Sons Ltd for extracts from the Everyman's Library edition of Plato, *Parmenides*, translated by John Warrington (London, 1961);

Walter Hamilton and Penguin Books Ltd for extracts from the Penguin Classics edition of Plato, *Phaedrus* (London, 1973);

Hugh Tredennick and Penguin Books Ltd for extracts from the Penguin Classics edition of Plato, *Phaedo* (London, 1954);

William Heinemann Ltd for the use of extracts from these books published in the Loeb Classical Library:

Plutarch, *Lives*, edited and translated by Bernadotte Perrin (1916); Thucydides, *The Peloponnesian Wars*, translated by C. Foster Smith; and Aristotle *The Politics*, translated by H. Rackham.

J. M. Dent & Sons Ltd for extracts from the Everyman's Library edition of Aristotle, *Metaphysics*, edited and translated by John Warrington (London, 1956).

Contents

List of Maps

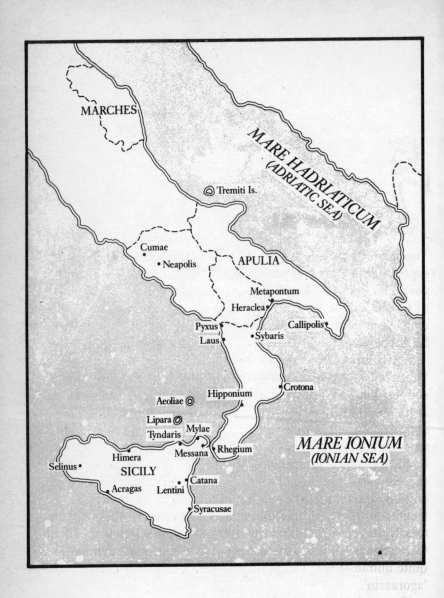

Fig. 1: **Magna Graecia**

reface

Dear Salvatore,[1]

You may not realize it, but you are a philosopher. You are a philosopher because the way you tackle life and its problems is personal to you. This being so, I believe that some knowledge about the History of Greek Philosophy could be useful to you, and that is why I have decided to write one especially. My aim will be to tell you in simple language about the lives and ideas of the earliest philosophers.

Why *Greek* philosophy? In the first place let me tell you, my dear Salvatore, that you are not really Italian at all, but Greek. I'm quite serious. You're Greek, and, I am tempted to add, 'Athenian'. Greece, as a way of life, is a very large Mediterranean land of sun and conversation which, as far as our own peninsula is concerned, extends more or less to the banks of the Volturno (see figure 1). Beyond this boundary, which is not only territorial but also temperamental, live the Romans, the Etruscans and the Central Europeans, peoples entirely different from us and who tend to be on a different wavelength. So that you may understand this essential difference more clearly, let me suggest that you consider a verb which is found in the Greek language but, having no equivalent in any other tongue, is quite untranslatable except by long and roundabout phrases. This is 'agorazein'.

'Agorazein' means 'to betake oneself to the market place to see

[1]Salvatore is the deputy-assistant porter at No. 58, Via Petrarca, where Professor Gennaro Bellavista lives (See *Thus Spake Bellavista*, Picador, 1988).

what people are saying', and therefore to chat, to buy, to sell and to meet one's friends. It also means to sally forth with no precise scope, to stroll about in the sunshine until dinner time, or in other words 'intalliarsi', as a Neapolitan would say, meaning to mooch round in a leisurely fashion until one becomes an integral part of the gesticulating, glance-exchanging, tongue-wagging human magma. In particular, the participle of this verb, 'agorazonta', describes the method of locomotion of one who practises 'agorazein': an easy stroll with hands clasped behind the back and rarely, if ever, in a straight line. A foreign tourist or businessman finding himself in a Greek city, be it Corinth or Pozzuoli, would be considerably puzzled by the sight of so many people strolling up and down the street, stopping every now and then to indulge in a brief, heated discussion and then strolling on only to stop again after a few paces. He would probably imagine that he had arrived on a public holiday, when in actual fact he is watching a perfectly normal scene of 'agorazein'. Greek philosophy owes a great deal to the peripatetic habits of the southern Mediterranean races.

> SOCRATES: My dear Phaedrus, where have you come from and where are you going?
> PHAEDRUS: I have been with Lysias, the son of Cephalus, Socrates, and now I am going for a walk outside the city walls. Our common friend, Acumenus, says that a country walk is more refreshing than a stroll through the city squares.

This is the opening passage of one of the finest of Plato's dialogues: the *Phaedrus*. To be honest, these Athenians did nothing one could call productive: they walked, they talked, they discussed the nature of Good and Evil, but as for work, as for getting down to producing something practical for sale or use, that was out of the question. On the other hand, we must bear in mind that while the citizens of Athens in those days numbered some 20,000, there was a second division of at least 200,000 consisting of slaves and metics,[2] so there was no shortage of people to do the work and keep things running

---

[2]Metics: foreigners permanently resident in Athens.

smoothly. And the Athenians, not yet infected by the virus of consumerism, were happy to live relatively simply and were therefore free to spend their time on intellectual pursuits and conversation.

But let's return to philosophy and the reason for my present undertaking.

Philosophy is an essential tool for human life, a useful aid in solving everyday problems, yet the study of it is not, unfortunately, compulsory like National Service.[3] If it were up to me I would make it part of the curriculum in all secondary schools; I fear, however, that the powers that be consider it outmoded and have largely replaced it with the more up-to-date subject of 'social sciences'. Which is rather like abolishing mathematics because greengrocers use automatic tills.

So, what is philosophy? Not an easy question to answer off the cuff. Man reached the highest peaks of civilization via two basic disciplines: science and religion. Now, while science, engaging our rational resources, studies the world around us, religion, responding to an instinctive human need, seeks something absolute, a kind of knowledge above and beyond the reach of the senses and intellect. Well, philosophy occupies a half-way house between the two, having more in common with one or the other, depending upon whether we are dealing with so-called rationalist philosophers or with those of a more mystical tendency. Bertrand Russell, who belonged to the rationalist school of thought, described philosophy as a kind of no man's land, occupying the middle ground between science and theology and vulnerable to attack from both sides.

You, my dear Salvatore, not having had any further education, know nothing whatsoever about philosophy. But that's nothing to be ashamed about: you are not alone. The truth is that no one knows anything about philosophy. In Italy, just to take an example, out of a population of 56 million, maybe 150,000 people might possibly be able to string together a couple of sentences about the essential differences between Plato and Aristotle – and these would be the teachers of philosophy and students currently sitting their exams. Most of the others, even those with a classical education, would only be able to talk about platonic love, defined as that kind of affectionate

[3] *Translator's note*: In Italy, National Service is still compulsory.

relationship between a man and a woman which unhappily stops short of going to bed together; Plato's own ideas on the subject were much more complex and much less inhibited.

If philosophy is a kind of 'black hole' in the cultural background of the average Italian, who or what is to blame for this? Not, in my opinion, the subject itself, which is neither dull nor difficult, but rather the specialists in the field who, deliberately and collectively, have decided that it should not be too widely available. Of course I cannot claim to have read every history of philosophy ever published, but in those that I have come across, with the one exception of Bertrand Russell's *History of Western Philosophy*, the academic jargon has always posed a serious obstacle. I sometimes suspect the authors of addressing themselves more to their colleagues than to students of the subject.

Technical jargon is a nuisance which has long bedevilled every branch of learning. The fact is that there have always been people around who have enjoyed mouthing their own mumbo-jumbo to impress the uninitiated. It began with the Egyptian priests five thousand years ago and continued with every kind of pettifogging wonder-worker you can think of up to and including the hospital doctors who, when they are interviewed on television, never say anything as simple as 'broken leg' but prefer to use the more sophisticated term 'fractured femur'.

Specialist terminology pays, it makes people feel important and increases the power of whoever uses it. There is no group, association or club today that does not have its own jargon. The bad habit knows no bounds. At Italian airports, for example, the phrase trotted out every time a plane is late runs: 'Due to the delayed arrival of the *aeromobile* (airliner), flight AZ642 will be et cetera et cetera'. I should love to ask the official who first worded that announcement if he would ever dream of using the same language when telling his wife in the privacy of his own home that he plans a trip by air. Would he say, 'Caterì, I have an appointment in Milan tomorrow morning and I shall take the *airliner* departing at 0900 hours'? He wouldn't, of course. Speaking to his wife he would use the ordinary word, keeping the other for the exclusive benefit of us poor travellers, well knowing that confronted with such an unusual term we are bound to be so intimidated that we will be totally unable to summon up the courage to complain about the delay. It's tantamount to being told: 'What can you poor ignoramuses be expected to know about delays! You don't know the first thing about aircraft! Shut up and be grateful that we deign to speak to you at all!'

And I'll give you some more examples. When cholera broke out in Naples, mussels were thought to be responsible. The normal Italian word for mussels is *cozze*, but because television newsreaders called them *mitili*, all Neapolitans, not having the foggiest idea what *mitili* were, went on happily eating *cozze*. A similar thing happened one day in the house of my tailor, Saverio Guardascione, while he and I were watching the news on television with Papiluccio, a mongrel he'd found wandering alone near the football stadium the day after the earthquake. The announcer said: 'The escaped convict was recaptured with the aid of canine auxiliars,' and Saverio asked me, 'Professò, what does he mean by *canine auxiliars*?' 'Dogs,' I replied, simplifying slightly. *'Gesù, Gesù!'* exclaimed Saverio. 'To think that I've had a canine auxiliar for over a year without knowing it!' Papiluccio sensed that he was being talked about and wagged his tail gratefully.

I hardly need say that politicians are the worst offenders of the lot. They are the quintessential practitioners of the art of using abstruse language for personal advantage. I once heard one of them say on television: 'Indubitably we in Italy suffer from a scarcity of fractional coinage which constitutes a problem now partially solved by the emission of fiduciary currency.' He meant that small change was in short supply so one got by with mini-cheques. Believe me, I would have had the man stripped on the spot and the right phrase beaten into him! The problem is that experts are always afraid that the use of simple language may be mistaken for ignorance. And heaven help you if these same experts feel that you are being too free and easy with their pet subject! They immediately dub you a 'popularizer' and sneer and wrinkle their noses up as if the word 'popularize' stank to high heaven. The truth is that such people feel no love for others and would rather inflate their ego than share their knowledge.

Italians are past masters at making culture boring. You only have to visit one of the museums to realize this: vast galleries, all identical and always unfrequented, sculptures and paintings displayed with no information, glum attendants just waiting for their pensions, sepulchral silence – of the crypt rather than the cemetery. What a contrast to American museums! Take, for example, the Museum of Natural History in New York. A place enjoyed by everyone, old and young, the scholar and the illiterate. There are bars, restaurants, video shows to explain the whys and wherefores, dioramas reconstructing prehistoric landscapes with dinosaurs grinding their teeth, and Red Indian canoes with Sitting Bull plying the paddle. I agree that this kind of museum reminds one more of Walt Disney than of Charles Darwin, but after spending a day there the visitor emerges having at least learnt something.

Bearing this in mind, I am now going to disregard all the scholars and pedants and show you just how entertaining and easy to understand Greek Philosophy can be. There are some philosophers in particular who, after you have got to know them a bit, will begin to strike you as so familiar that you will end up by seeing similarities between them and your friends and relations. You may even find that to describe the mentality of people as Aristotelian, Platonist, Sophist, Sceptic, Epicurean, Cynic, Cyrenaic and so on is more effective than to refer to the signs of the zodiac. It cannot be denied: we are the direct descendants of these gentlemen! When the Trojan Wars ended, in 1184 BC,[4] the Greek heroes and Trojan refugees were scattered, some by storms on the return journey, others by fear of revenge, and they dotted the shores of the Mediterranean with villages and settlements thus becoming the precursors of our own ancestors. In the succeeding centuries, the Peloponnese and Attica were regularly invaded by barbarian hordes from the North and the Greeks, beginning to feel overcrowded, decided to take to their ships and go off to found elsewhere replicas of their own *poleis*, or cities, each having its own temple, agora (central square), theatre, prytaneum (civic centre), gymnasium and so on. We can already see from what has been said so far that Ancient Greece did much the same for the development of Western ideas as the Big Bang, the

---

[4]The date of the fall of Troy – by no means certain – is derived from an obscure calculation made by Eratosthenes.

explosion that produced the galaxies and constellations, did for the development of the Universe. If Greek civilization had never existed, we should have fallen under the influence of oriental doctrines, and that, believe me my dear Salvatore, would have been no joke! If you doubt my word, look at the map and you will see, just below Greece and a little bit to the right of the Mediterranean, the terrifying Middle East, a strange land where everyone is infected with religious mania from earliest childhood. Had a couple of battles not been fought and fortunately won by our side (that of Plataea against the Persians and that of Poitiers against the Muslims)[5] and without the strong influence of Greek rational thought inherited from the old pre-Socratic philosophers, none of us would have escaped from the Asiatic offensive, and perhaps at midday today we should all have been kneeling with our behinds in the air and our faces to the ground towards Mecca. However, the ancient *poleis* were not, thanks be, governed by priests as was the case in Egypt and Assyria, but by groups of aristocrats with little taste for prayers and mysticism. But having mentioned religion, let's have a quick look at the relations between the Greeks and their Gods.

In the first place, the Gods were not omnipotent. Not even Zeus, the Father of the Gods, could do exactly as he pleased. The sovereign power over him and all the other Gods was Fate, or, as Homer tells us, *Ananke*, Necessity. This limitation of the power of the Gods, and of tyrants in general, is part of the great democratic tradition we inherited from our forefathers. For Greek philosophers Good was identified with Moderation.

In the second place, Greek religion was not excessively religious. The Gods were prey to practically every mortal weakness: they squabbled, got drunk, told lies, slept around and so on. So it is hardly surprising if the people's respect for them was, as a result, somewhat modified. They were honoured certainly, but only so far. This was nothing compared to the terror inspired by Jahve, the terrible God of the Hebrews. Take the seat of the Gods, Olympus, for example: not

---

[5]For those who cannot resist the seduction of erudite minutiae, the Battle of Plataea was fought in 479 BC and was won by a Greek legion commanded by Pausanias, while that of Poitiers was fought in AD 732 and provided a crucial victory for Charles Martel.

situated up in the sky as in the case of all serious religions, but at the top of a mountain, an indication that the Greeks were not the slightest bit bothered at the thought of anyone going up there to carry out a spot check.

The reason for dwelling on the religion of Ancient Greece is that the birth of philosophy coincided precisely with the period when superstition and Orphic rites were giving way to the first scientific observations of nature. It was no mere fluke that Thales of Miletus, an astronomer who specialized in solar eclipses, was the first philosopher in history – always provided that we exclude any Tom, Dick or Harry who was able to formulate a thought not directly related to his most immediate material needs, in which case we would have to put the birth of philosophy back by at least 40,000 years to the Palaeolithic era.

I can imagine it happening like this: Hunu was in a happy frame of mind that evening because everything had gone right: he had killed a young deer, tender and fleshy, quartered it with his flint axe and roasted it slowly over the fire. He and Hana, his woman, had both eaten until they could eat no more. After their meal they had made love and Hana had then withdrawn to the cave, leaving Hunu outside, alone with his thoughts. The night was very hot and he had no desire for sleep so he stretched himself at full length on the grass and lay there looking up at the starry sky. It was a moonless August night. Thousands upon thousands of tiny points of light twinkled above his head. What, Hunu asked himself, could those points of fire be? Who lit them and hung them up there in the sky? An enormous giant? A God? . . . Thus were religion and science born at the same time, from the fear of the unknown and the need to know. And hence philosophy.

L. De Crescenzo

Author's Note

From my first days in primary school I loved break times; at secondary school I looked forward with eager anticipation to games and R.E., and in later life, during conferences or meetings, I greeted the ten o'clock coffee break with a sigh of relief. With this in mind, I felt it was only right to create space among the Greek philosophers for some of 'my' philosophers, men with somewhat unexpected names like Peppino Russo and Tonino Capone: they are the break times that I offer to my readers. My publisher, for his part, fearing that some unwary student might mistake them for real philosophers and quote them in an examination paper, decided to accord them a different typeface and even give them a border.

I
The Seven Sages

The Seven Sages numbered twenty-two and were as follows: Thales, Pittacus, Bias, Solon, Cleobulus, Chilon, Periander, Myson, Aristodemus, Epimenides, Leophantus, Pythagoras, Anacharsis, Epicharmus, Acusilaus, Orpheus, Pisistratus, Pherecydes, Chabrinus of Hermione, Lasos, Pamphilus and Anaxagoras.

There's nothing very surprising about the fact that so many Sages are named in the sacred books: the reason is simply that the historians of philosophy never managed to agree about whom to include. To be fair, they agreed about the first four, Thales, Pittacus, Bias and Solon (who might therefore be considered the key players of the team), but when it came to making the side up to seven they had at least eighteen reserves to call on. Apart from anything else, there was always someone ready to make an illegal substitution when no one was looking and slip in a friend, maybe even a prominent politician, much as if I, having been asked to compile a list of the Seven Sages today, were to include the Prime Minister for the sake of flattery.

Joking apart, I do believe I once met a real Sage. His name was Alfonso and he was the proprietor of a billiard saloon in Fuorigrotta. Firstly, and most importantly, he looked the part, being of venerable age, bearded, white-haired and taciturn. He hardly ever spoke, and when he did so his words were few, cold, concise and final. Every now and then a player would ask him to establish a point and he would approach the billiard table, look at the balls as if he had seen them lying just so many times before, and simply say 'white' or 'red'. Nothing else. You might well ask me how on earth I can call him a

Sage without ever hearing him speak. I just know, or rather I just sense it. In Don Alfonso's eyes there was a lifetime of experience, the expression of a man who had seen it all and been through everything. Had I ever been in trouble, I am convinced that I could have gone to him and found comfort. Perhaps, as when looking at the billiard balls, he would have remained silent for a few seconds and then, with a single word, shed light.

The Sages, too, were all men of few words: laconic, as one might say. 'Knowing, keep silence' (Solon), 'Shun the hasty word' (Bias), 'Be avid to listen but not to speak' (Cleobulus), 'Let not your tongue outrun your thought' (Chilon) are all sayings which give the impression of an age when wisdom and reticence went hand in hand. For their gift of succinctness perhaps we should dub the Sages the inventors of the proverb. Many of their maxims are still in use: Cleobulus' 'Mate with one of your own rank' corresponds to the Italian saying *moglie e buoi dei paesi tuoi*[1] and 'Choose well whom you deal with' is the equivalent of the Neapolitan proverb *Fattelle cu chi è cchiù meglio 'e te e fanne 'e spese.*[2]

Thanks to their axioms or wise sayings, the fame of the Seven Sages spread from one place to another until, even without the help of the mass media, everyone in the Greek world knew all about Thales and his companions. Their axioms were used by fathers for the education of their sons and orators quoted them liberally in their speeches both before the assembly and in the tribunal. Their songs were sung at banquets and were, in contrast to the offerings at the Eurovision Song Contest, endowed with high moral content. A song of Chilon's I particularly remember has the refrain: 'By the whetstone gold is tried . . . and by gold is the mind of men brought to the test.'[3]

The most likeable of the twenty-two is, in my opinion, Pittacus of Mytilene. Diogenes Laertius tells us that he was not only a wise man but also an admirable *strategos* (military or naval commander), and that when he gave up office the people of Mytilene presented him with a large tract of land and christened it Pittacia in his honour; but

---

[1]'Take your wife and your oxen from your own neighbourhood!'
[2]'Deal with your superiors and you will pay for it.'
[3]Diogenes Laertius, *Lives of Eminent Philosophers* I 71.

Pittacus, having no desire to become a great landowner, accepted only as much of the land as was necessary to supply his own needs, justifying his decision by declaring that 'the half was more than the whole'.[4]

Here are some of the most striking maxims of Pittacus of Mytilene[5]: 'Do not announce your plans beforehand, for if they fail you will be ridiculed'; 'It is hard to be good'; 'The earth is trustworthy, the sea untrustworthy'; and, most striking of all, 'Suffer minor disturbances from your neighbour'. This last saying could well be considered the Neapolitans' eleventh commandment, seeing that it exalts their most obvious virtue: tolerance. Only tolerance makes it possible to accept the corollary: 'Feel free to disturb your neighbour', which in point of fact is not so much a maxim as a serious inconvenience for everyone who happens to live in these parts.

There is a story told about the Seven Sages that is too illuminating and entertaining for us even to want to check its authenticity. One day, apparently, the seven wise men decided to take a trip into the countryside and all agreed to meet at Delphi at the shrine of the Oracle of Apollo; here they were received with all due honour by the eldest of the priests who, seeing the flower of Greek wisdom gathered around him, immediately decided to turn the occasion to account by inviting each one to carve a saying on the temple wall. The first to agree to this was Chilon of Sparta,[6] who got himself a ladder and wrote over the main door the famous phrase 'Know thyself'.[7] One by one the others followed suit. Cleobulus and Periander, one to the right and the other to the left of the main entrance, wrote their celebrated epigrams: 'Moderation is best' and 'Tranquillity is the most beautiful thing in the world'. Solon, out of modesty, chose a dark little corner in the peristyle and wrote 'Learn to obey and you will learn to command'. Thales inscribed his words on the outer walls of the temple so that pilgrims approaching the shrine along the Sacred Path should be able, as soon as they had rounded the corner of the altar of Chios, to read: 'Remember your friends!' Pittacus, ever

[4]Diogenes Laertius, *op. cit.* I 75.
[5]Diogenes Laertius, *op. cit.* I 76–78.
[6]Diogenes Laertius, *op. cit.* I 40–42.
[7]Several authorities have attributed the saying to Thales.

the eccentric, knelt down at the foot of the Python's tripod and sculpted the obscure phrase 'Restore what has been entrusted to you'. When these had all done, the only one remaining was Bias of Priene, and much to everyone's surprise he drew back, muttering that he didn't feel like it, and ... actually ... didn't know what to write. The others gathered round him and made suggestions but in spite of their encouragement Bias seemed determinedly reluctant. The more they said, 'Come on, Bias, son of Teutames, you who are the wisest of us all, leave a trace of your illumination for future visitors to the shrine,' the more he warded them off, saying: 'Listen, my friends, it would be much better if I were to write nothing.' They argued and argued, and eventually wore the poor sage down to the point when he could refuse no longer, and it was then that he reached for the stylus with a trembling hand and wrote: 'Most men are bad'.[8]

Read in haste, the phrase seems harmless enough, and yet this apophthegm of Bias' represents the most dramatic judgement ever expressed in Greek philosophy. 'Most men are bad' is a bomb capable of destroying any ideology. It's like going into a supermarket and taking a tin of baked beans from the bottom of a great pyramid of tins of baked beans: they all fall down. The very principle of democracy is here undermined, universal suffrage, Marxism, Christianity and every other doctrine based upon love of one's neighbour. Jean Jacques Rousseau, who held that all men are by nature good, loses game, set and match to Thomas Hobbes with his *homo homini lupus*.

I know that our self-pride naturally refuses to accept the pessimism of Bias, yet, deep down, the suspicion stirs that maybe the old madman was right. Anyone who has been to a football match knows what a crowd is really like. And in Ancient Rome, not chance but common sense put the fate of the defeated gladiator into the hands of the Emperor alone and never into those of the spectators, for the mass would invariably have given the 'thumbs down'. The *civis romanus* went along to the Colosseum with his entire family precisely in order to see as many men killed as possible, and this – making all due allowances – is still true today. That man is the cruellest of all living things is not, I think, a matter for debate. The only one who

---

[8]Diogenes Laertius, *op. cit.* I 88.

holds out some hope for us is Bergson by saying that humanity, slowly but surely, is improving. Let us be thankful for such a ray of hope and look forward eagerly to the year 3000.

There is another possible interpretation of Bias' apophthegm: that most men are bad when acting *en masse.* In other words, single human beings may be good individually, and only become transformed into wild animals when acting as a mass. I don't know about you, gentle reader, but I have always had a tendency to ally myself with minorities, and I must now ask myself why. Have I avoided the crowd for fear of being corrupted by collective evil, or could the opposite be the case, and I have done so in order to give a freer rein to my own ill will in respect of the masses? Is it sheer snobbery? A fear of becoming one of the herd? An antidemocratic racism typical of those who believe themselves to belong to a small, select band? The answer to this question might be deeply humiliating.

In the fifth century BC an anonymous Athenian, possibly a refugee or an outcast, wrote a pamphlet[9] purporting to be a discussion between two citizens airing their opinions uninhibitedly about the new democratic regime in Athens. One says: '. . . in the best men you find the minimum of unruliness and injustice, and the maximum inclination towards goodness; whereas among the masses you find the maximum degree of ignorance, disorderliness and wickedness, given that poverty induces ignominy and from this comes the unmannerliness and brutality that have their source in indigence . . .

This passage is probably the earliest criticism of the democratic system, and it is interesting to note that the author, although a dyed-in-the-wool reactionary, does not blame the people who, he says, 'try to help each other', as much as those who 'although they are not themselves of the people, choose to operate in a city governed by the masses rather than by the best because they know that their own lasciviousness will be better concealed here than in an oligarchy'.

To return to the Seven Sages, one thing I have learnt is that we should always be slightly wary when dealing with wisdom, for it is

---

[9]This document was found among the works of Xenophon, who was a friend of the Thirty Tyrants and therefore an enemy of Athenian democracy. It was published in Italy by Sellerio in 1982 as *La democrazia come violenza.*

often deliberately at variance with idealism. Wisdom is no more than common sense, a sound knowledge about the world, whereas idealism is the irresistible desire to believe in a better future. Wisdom speaks of men as they really are, idealism imagines them as they could be. Two different ways of looking at the world, and the choice is up to you.

II
Miletus

iletus today is a small Turkish town on the Anatolian coast, just south of the island of Samos. During the seventh and sixth centuries BC it was the most important town in Ionia and perhaps in the whole world. It may never have occurred to you, but the focal point of history, and hence of the arts, of literature and of military power, has a habit of shifting itself very slowly over the face of the globe more or less following the same path as the sun: originating on the western Asiatic coast, it paused for quite some time in Greece and then leapt over to Rome where, what with the Roman Empire and the Papacy, it hung around for a few centuries before emigrating first to France, then England, and then doing another leap over to America, where it seems to have settled for the time being. Tomorrow it will continue on to Japan and maybe, after another thousand years or so, we shall see it again around these parts.

Miletus was founded before the year one thousand BC by settlers who may have come from Crete or from the Greek mainland or could even have been, as some maintain, refugees fleeing from the nearby city of Troy when it was burnt to the ground a few years previously. According to Herodotus, the most imaginative of all the ancient Greek historians, the invaders 'took no women with them but married Carian girls whose parents they had killed'.[1] It may have been the usual story of the Rape of the Sabine Women to whom heaven knows how many peoples of today owe their existence. Apparently the head

[1]Herodotus, *The Histories* I 146.

Fig. 2: **The Ionian Coast**

of this band of ravishers was no less than the son of Poseidon, Neleus. This should come as no surprise if we remember that ancient peoples were in the habit of ascribing to the gods all the disgraceful crimes committed by their ancestors. Shame that America and Russia cannot treat events in Chile and Afghanistan the same way.

An important fact to bear in mind for the purposes of the story I am about to relate is that Miletus was a modern city where commerce was highly developed and where the only God who really counted was that of Money. Very much the same as in New York today.

The narrow borderland of the Ionian coast (see fig. 2) lay like the ham in a sandwich between Greece and the Persian Empire, its many villages and towns taking advantage of this and trading with both sets of neighbours. And none more than Miletus, from whose harbours ships came and went laden with all the bounty of the earth: grain, oil, metals, papyri, wine and perfume. Now, as is so often the case in periods of thriving prosperity, the Milesians tended to lose interest in the mystical abstractions of religion, preferring to occupy themselves with more rational activities. So this was the moment when interest in nature, astronomy and the art of navigation first surfaced, in a city which we can imagine as a sun-drenched hive of activity, bustling with sailors, merchants and businessmen.

Come with me for a short walk through the ancient city of Miletus to the little hill of Kalabak Tepe, just high enough to get a good view of the whole city.

The city (see fig. 3) stretches below us along a short peninsula. The streets are narrow and cross each other at right angles. On a different scale, this could almost be Manhattan. Over there, to our left, we can see the 'Theatre' harbour and, a bit nearer, the 'Lion' harbour. A long line of Phrygian slaves carry bundles of papyri towards the western market. The market-place itself is alive with people chatting, bartering at the tops of their voices and laughing. All the signs are that this is a wealthy, carefree society.

Unfortunately, this state of affairs did not last. The geographical position that was once Miletus' key to prosperity eventually proved fatal. One black day, in spite of having made an alliance with the Lydians, Miletus was attacked by the Persian hordes under Darius and razed to the ground. 'Most of the men were killed by the

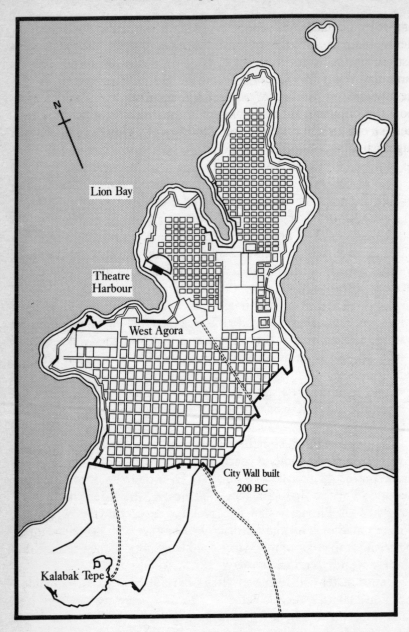

Fig. 3: Miletus

long-haired Persians and the women and children were made slaves,' Herodotus tells us, adding: 'The Athenians showed their profound distress at the capture of Miletus in a number of ways, and in particular, when Phrynichus produced his play, *The Capture of Miletus*, the audience in the theatre burst into tears. The author was fined a thousand drachmas for reminding them of a disaster which touched them so closely and they forbade anybody ever to put the play on the stage again.'[2]

[2]Herodotus, *op. cit.* VI 18–21.

III

Thales

hales was a Milesian with a sound grasp of engineering. He was born in the second half of the seventh century BC, the son of a Phoenician couple.[1] As soon as he attained the age of reason, he boarded the first outward bound ship and began a long series of voyages between Egypt and the Middle East. Practically speaking, it was the Egyptian and Chaldean priests who educated him and taught him everything that was known at the time about astronomy, mathematics and the art of navigation.

When Thales returned to his homeland, his mother, mistress Cleobulina, wanted him to settle down at once and tried, as mothers will, to find him a wife. But there was no way she could persuade him. Thales was different from all the other young men. When asked why he did not marry, he always replied: 'It is not yet time', until the day when he changed tack and answered 'It is too late'. And when he was asked why he had no children he replied, 'because he loved children'.[2] So you see Thales was a philosopher, even though the word had not yet been invented. The word 'philosopher' only acquired currency with Pythagoras and not until the time of Plato did philosophy attain the dignity of a profession. So Thales, as far as his Milesian contemporaries were concerned, was simply a rather strange individual with his head in the clouds. 'Such a nice chap,' they would say, 'but no common sense.' And they would continue: 'Maybe he knows a

[1]Diogenes Laertius, *op. cit.* IX I 22.
[2]Diogenes Laertius, *op. cit.* IX I 26.

lot, but as he never has a penny to his name, what good is it to him?' Even his slave-girl made fun of him, apparently, because once when he fell into a pothole while looking at the stars, she teased him unmercifully:[3] 'O Thales,' she said, 'always so concerned with what is up in the sky yet you can't see what is right in front of you!' Now we don't know if the serving-girl Thales had before him was pretty or not, but we do know that he never showed much interest either in everyday matters or in women. He was, in other words, the prototype of the absent-minded scientist, capable of understanding five theorems of geometry at a time but rarely washing and totally incapable of organizing his own life. That he was not entirely devoid of practical ability is, however, shown by an anecdote told by Aristotle. One day, when Thales was sick and tired of the endless ribbing, he said, 'I'll show you!'[4] And calculating that there would be a bumper olive harvest the next year, he rented all the olive-presses he could find at a very low cost and when people were crying out for them he was able to sublet them on his own terms. We call this kind of speculation stock-jobbing and regard it as rather underhand, but Thales used it simply to prove that, *if he wanted to*, a philosopher was quite able to amass riches however and whenever he chose. In fact Thales was as crafty as they come and well deserved Plato's description of him as an 'ingenious inventor of techniques'. During the war between the Lydians and the Persians, the troops under Croesus were unable to cross the river Halys, so Thales, sound engineer that he was, diverted part of the water in such a way that both streams became fordable.[5]

His real fame as a scientist came, however, from his predicting the eclipse of the sun in 585 BC. To be honest, this was more of a lucky guess than a scientific calculation. Thales had learned from the Chaldean priests that eclipses occurred more or less regularly every ninety years, and this was the basis for his prediction. We now know that the accurate prediction of an eclipse can only be made by a very much more complex calculation, and that while an eclipse of the sun

[3]Plato, *Theaetetus*, 174a.
[4]Aristotle, *Politics* I 3, 1259a.
[5]Herodotus, *op. cit.* I 75.

by the moon may be total in Chaldea it may only be partial two thousand kilometres away in Anatolia. At most, Thales should have told his fellow citizens to look out of the window from time to time because they might just be lucky enough to see an eclipse. Instead of which he insisted on, and by great good fortune got, a total eclipse – an event which frightened the life out of everyone in the region and even put a stop to the war between the Lydians and the Persians.[6] From that day on his reputation grew by leaps and bounds and for Thales this meant that he could dedicate himself to his studies in greater tranquillity. He measured the height of the pyramids[7] by comparing the length of the shadow they cast with the shadow cast by an object whose height he already knew, and, by a further application of the principles of geometry, succeeded in calculating the distance between the coast and ships at sea. He also divided the year into 365 days[8] and was the first to observe Ursa Minor and establish its importance to navigation. Callimachus dedicated these lines to him:[9]

> *And it was said of him that he observed*
> *the starry constellation of the Bear*
> *by which the Phoenician sailors steered their ships.*

He left nothing in writing. A book on navigation thought to have been written by Thales was later proved to have been the work of one Phocus of Samos. He died from the effects of heat, thirst and, above all, the crowd, while watching an athletic contest at the stadium. When everybody had left, he was found lying on the steps as if asleep. He was very old. Diogenes commemorated his death with this epigram:

> *As Thales watched the games one festal day,*
> *The fierce sun smote him, and he passed away;*

[6]Herodotus, *op. cit.* I 74.
[7]Pliny, *Naturalis historia* XXXVI 82.
[8]Diogenes Laertius, *op. cit.* IX I 27.
[9]Callimachus, *Iambus* I, vv. 54–5.

Zeus, thou didst well to raise him: his dim eyes
No longer could behold the starry skies.[10]

When I was at secondary school, I thought our official textbook for philosophy too difficult by half, so I got by – like all my mates, I hasten to add – with the help of the Bignami cribs. For those who have never encountered either cribs or Bignami, I should explain that these are little books containing only the bare bones of a given subject; they form, as it were, a kind of *Reader's Digest* of schoolboy learning. The Bignami cribs for history, philosophy, chemistry and indeed everything else under the sun are naturally not very popular with teachers, but lazy schoolchildren throughout Italy should, sooner or later, erect a monument to Professor Bignami in token of eternal gratitude.

When matriculation exams loomed (I speak of exams as they used to be), I found myself up against the problem of revising three years' work across the board, and at that point even the tiny Bignami volumes seemed too detailed, so I fell back on the age-old system of outlines and notes. In a black-covered exercise book with squared paper I jotted down summaries of all I had gathered from reading Bignami, thus obtaining a summary of a summary of the things I had to remember. I mention all this simply because in my old exercise book, which I still treasure, I have found but a single phrase relating to Thales: 'Thales – the water one'. Well now, if there is one way to belittle Thales' contribution to the history of philosophy, it is by reducing him to the mere originator of the theory that water is the basic substance of matter. But let me explain.

Thales had observed that every living thing contains moisture. Plants contain moisture, all foodstuffs contain moisture and even seeds contain moisture, whereas rocks are dry and cadavers very soon desiccate.[11] His favourite phrase was: 'Water is the most beautiful thing in the world'. We should not forget, among other things, that Thales had spent his most formative years in arid zones such as Egypt and Mesopotamia, where water-cults were widespread, partly owing to the fact that agriculture and the very survival of the population

[10]Diogenes Laertius, *op. cit.* IX I 39.
[11]Aristotle, *Metaphysics* I 3, 983b 21.

depended upon the flooding of the rivers. It comes as no surprise to find the Egyptians worshipping the Nile as a God. I am convinced, however, that Thales' equation of water and life is the expression of a much more complex thesis than the simple observation that water is present in all living things. He held water, or rather moisture, to be the soul of the world, the universal essence. Aetios, in a passage relating to Thales, said: 'A divine power is present in the element of water by which it is endowed with movement.'[12]

The Milesian school, of which Thales is chronologically the first representative, is characterized by this search for the primordial element, the *archè* as the Greeks termed it, from which everything arose. Thales held that the *archè* was water because water, besides being a liquid, becomes a solid when frozen and a gas when boiled.

Thales imagined the earth itself as floating upon an enormous expanse of water[13] like a huge raft which pitched from time to time provoking earthquakes.[14] The idea of the world resting upon something was not new in popular mythology: there were those, like the Greeks, who held that it rested upon the shoulders of Atlas, others, like the Hindus, that it was supported by an elephant who stood upon the back of a tortoise. Woe betide anyone if they should ask a Hindu what the tortoise was standing on, though.

As well as his theories about water, Thales also asserted that everything had a soul and was therefore 'full of gods'.[15] When speaking on this subject he used to produce a nail and a magnet from his pocket and show his astounded fellow citizens how 'stone could move iron'.[16]

To summarize, then, Thales' place in the history of philosophy is an important one, not so much for the answers he gave to various questions as for the fact that he asked the questions in the first place. To look around one, to ponder, to refrain from looking to the gods for the solution of every mystery, this was the first step taken by Western thought towards the interpretation of the universe.

[12]Aetios, I 7, 11.
[13]Aristotle, *De Coelo* II, 13, 294a 30–3.
[14]Seneca, *Naturales Quaestiones* III 14.
[15]Aristotle, *De Anima* I 5, 411a 8.
[16]Aristotle, *De Anima* I 2, 405a 20–2.

IV
Anaximander

naximander was a pupil of Thales and possibly a relation too. He was born in Miletus in 610 BC and was therefore about twenty years younger than his teacher. The history of civilization accords him the distinction of having been the first to produce a map.[1] In those days seafaring was a hazardous matter undertaken with great temerity and very few safety measures: there were as yet no compasses, no sextants and no navigation charts. The best one could do was wait for good weather, at least for the start of the voyage, and the blessing of the oracle at Didyma. In such circumstances, the maps produced by Anaximander must have represented the epitome of progress to the merchants of the time, especially since the philosopher filled them with advice and information about the various peoples likely to be encountered during the voyage.

It is said of Anaximander that he was the inventor of the *gnomon*, or sundial,[2] and that his prediction of an earthquake in Sparta saved the lives of many Lacedaemonians.[3] Not much is known about his life. From his ability as a cartographer we can deduce that he travelled a great deal as did all the pre-Socratic philosophers. Xenophanes, according to his own account, travelled the world for sixty-seven years and Democritus boasted of having seen more different races and

[1]Diogenes Laertius, *op. cit.* II 2.
[2]Favorinus of Arles mentions a quadrant designed by Anaximander for the agora in Sparta, from the centre of which a pole cast a shadow that moved across the ground according to the time of day.
[3]Cicero, *De divinatione* I 50, 112.

visited more unexplored parts of the world than any other man of his time.[4] As for Anaximander, as a young man he apparently founded a colony on the shores of the Black Sea called Apollonia in honour of the god.[5] I must make it clear at this point, however, that 'colonies' in this context have nothing to do with colonialism, least of all in its modern sense. There is no question here of an imperial power making militiary conquests. It was simply a case of landing with one's household goods and chattels in some uninhabited bay and settling down. The Greeks founded more than fifteen hundred such colonies in the Mediterranean area alone, disseminating their ways and their ideas as far afield as the coasts of France and Spain. We even hear of a certain Colaeus who, running before a storm and being driven right out of the Mediterranean through the Pillars of Hercules, settled on the Atlantic seaboard.[6]

There are, unfortunately, none of the amusing anecdotes about Anaximander that enliven the story of Thales – apart from one which shows him in the role of a singer. The story goes that one day, noticing some children who were laughing at his singing out of tune in the chorus, the philosopher turned to his companions saying, 'Gentlemen, we must do better or these children will give us a hard time!'[7]

Anaximander wrote about many subjects – nature, the earth, the fixed stars, the sphere and others – but practically nothing has survived apart from four fragments and one phrase that must have tested many historians of philosophy. Here it is: 'The material cause and first element of things was the Infinite . . . and into that from which things take their rise they pass away once more, of necessity, for they make reparation and satisfaction to one another for their injustice according to the ordering of time'.[8]

Anaximander is stating here that the life principle of the universe is not water, as Thales believed, but an indefinite substance which he

[4]J. Burckhardt, *History of Greek Culture*, p. 321.
[5]Aelian, *Various History* III 17.
[6]Herodotus, *op. cit.* IV 152.
[7]Diogenes Laertius, *op. cit.* II 2.
[8]Simplicius, *Commentary on the Physics of Aristotle* 24, 13 (quoted in the English translation of J. Burnet in *Early Greek Philosophy*, p. 52).

calls *apeiron*, from which everything arises and to which everything returns. His teacher, he said, had got it wrong, because if any one of the four elements of Water, Air, Earth and Fire had been the primary substance the others would have ceased to be. In other words, Anaximander was convinced that Water, Air, Earth and Fire were finite elements all subject to some super-element, some Big Brother invisible to the naked eye.

The second part of the utterance now becomes clearer. Whenever one of the finite elements 'commits an injustice' towards any other by encroaching upon its territory, the super-element, the *apeiron*, drives it back to within its natural confines. So Anaximander thought of the elements as gods always ready to attack their own opposites: the Warm ever ready to encroach upon the Cold, the Dry upon the Moist and vice versa, but each prevented from gaining the upper hand by the restraining force of necessity. Justice in this context clearly means only respect for territory, but the poetic tone of the fragment prompts us to see more in it than a simple balance between the elements; words like 'reparation' and 'necessity', in particular, show that the philosopher was reaching towards some mystic concept of supreme order.

Even more striking is Anaximander's theory about the origin of the universe. In the words of Plutarch:[9]

He says that something capable of begetting Hot and Cold out of the Eternal was separated off at the origin of this world. From this arose a sphere of flame which fitted close round the air, surrounding the earth as the bark round a tree. When this had been torn off and shut up in certain rings, the sun, moon and stars came into existence.

So, to recapitulate, in the beginning there was only *apeiron*, the infinite substance, then Heat and Cold separated off, one forming the outer layer and the other the core of the universe and giving rise respectively to the Dry and the Moist. These last two, in good family tradition, continued to fight each other: in summer the Dry had the upper hand, snatching away vast quantities of sea water and transforming it into vapour, and in winter the Moist state regained its losses

[9]Pseudo-Plutarch, *Stromateis* 2.

by forming the vapour into clouds and restoring it to the earth as rain or snow. The *apeiron* supervised all this and ensured that neither prevailed ultimately over the other.[10] And let us hope, say I, that this state of affairs will continue well into the future and that Heat, in the guise of some nuclear horror, never prevails over the Cold which, in context, would mean ourselves and our homes.

The alternation of Heat and Cold is not simply a seasonal matter: almost every manifestation of the human soul itself oscillates between periods of activity and repose. All forms of creativity – art, music, fashion and many others – are subject to the influence of the moment and pass continually between phases which could be called 'still' and 'bubbly'. The temperature of succeeding generations goes up and down like the hemline of women's dresses. Look at our own century, for example: a 'hot' generation, that of Fascism, was followed by a 'cool', quiet, hard-working one, a constructive generation to which I am proud to belong. There was hardly time to draw breath, however, before the appearance of the youth movements of '68 – a generation for which the adjective 'boiling' would be an understatement! That was a high tide; today we are experiencing the ebb. I fear for the next. We can only hope and pray!

To return to Anaximander, let's see what the advocate of *apeiron* taught about how the world was made. He said that the Earth was a great column, or cylinder, with a girth many times its height (a kind of cake), suspended in air at the centre of the universe.[11] He said that it stays where it is because, being exactly in the centre, there is no reason why it should move in any one direction rather than any other. The width of the cake is three times its height and it is made of stone.[12] Immense wheels of fire rotate around the earth inside hoops of compressed air; on the internal rim of each one, where the spokes would be attached, there are, instead, holes – or rather openings like the end of a tube – through which we catch glimpses of the flaming mantle on the other side of the hoop of air. The stars are not, therefore, the fiery bodies that they appear to be, but only sparks of

[10]Aristotle, *Meteorologica* II 359b 6–11.
[11]Hippolytus, *Refutation of all Heresies* I 6, 1–7.
[12]Aetios, III 10, 2.

the Fire which surrounds the vault of the sky glimpsed through the 'holes' in the wheels. The diameter of the sun is twenty-seven times greater than that of the earth, while that of the moon is only nineteen times greater.

Anaximander taught that Man made his first appearance on the earth covered with scales and in a watery substance, a kind of mud, and that since the terrestrial climate was hostile to life, he was incubated throughout infancy in the mouths of a variety of animals very like fishes, whence he eventually emerged, shed his scales and began an independent existence.[13] These and other theories besides have been attributed to him by historians, but Anaximander's greatest merit lies in his having perceived the possibility of there being in the universe something supreme, sometimes called *apeiron*, sometimes Necessity, that 'encompasses and supports everything'[14] – which makes him at one and the same time a mystic philosopher and a cosmologist.

The theory I like best, however, is that of the stars being points of light glimpsed through the holes in the wheels. That I find enormously appealing. Among other things, it reminds me of Alberto Cammarano, an old friend of my father's who specialized in statues of the saints, angels' heads and Christmas cribs. Don Alberto made them throughout the year and sold them at Christmas from his tiny workshop in Via San Gregorio Armeno. He taught me all the tricks of his trade.

'My child, if you want a sky that looks just as it did on the night Jesus was born, you must get a sheet of Bristol-board, a kind of cardboard that lets no light through at all. Then you must paint it blue, but a dark blue, mind, like the paper they use for wrapping up macaroni! On the wall behind the cardboard you must put some little lights, three or four depending on the size of the base. The bulbs must be pearly white to diffuse the light better. Then, and this is the real secret, you must make little holes in the painted cardboard with a pin, as many holes as you want stars. And watch out, because this is vital, not to make the holes too big: they must be tiny, almost invisible,

---

[13]Aetios, V 19, 4.
[14]Aristotle, *Physics* IV 203b 4–15.

then the light will be refracted by the edge of the holes and shine through all broken up into hundreds of tiny rays. Then you will think that you really are in Bethlehem on the first Christmas night, it will be cold and you will hear the shepherds' pipes in the distance.'

V
Anaximenes

naximenes, a native of Miletus like the others, is a less important philosopher than his two predecessors, as even his name, which sounds like a diminutive of Anaximander, seems to suggest. One has to admit, however, that he lived in very difficult times, when the fortunes of Miletus were at their lowest ebb. In one of his letters to Pythagoras he writes: 'You are fortunate to be in Italy. You have become a favourite with the Crotonians and pupils flock to you even from Sicily ... Here we are threatened by the King of the Medes. How can you expect Anaximenes to pursue his study of the stars in peace and quiet when he is haunted by the spectres of destruction and slavery?'[1]

He wrote a book called *De Natura* of which only a fragment, as usual, survives. It runs: 'Just as our soul, being air, holds us together, so do breath and air encompass the whole world.'[2]

Not wanting to fall out with either Thales or Anaximander, Anaximenes produced a theory which, though apparently original, is substantially a combination of the teaching of his two predecessors: in taking air as the primordial substance he chose an element that occurs naturally, like Thales' water, but which also has the property of being invisible, like Anaximander's *apeiron*.

The following are the most important statements made by Anaximenes:

[1] Diogenes Laertius, *op. cit.* II 5.
[2] Aetios, I 3, 4.

- The universe is made of air and is subject to two spontaneous pro-
cesses: rarefaction and condensation.
- Fire is air in its most rarefied state; clouds, water, mud, earth and even
stones are air which has become progressively condensed.[3]
- The elements in nature differ from each other not in quality but in
quantity, all being formed from the same substance.
- Rarefaction produces Heat and ultimately Fire; condensation produces
Cold and ultimately Water; thus Heat and Cold are the effects rather than
the causes of the transformation of air.[4]

The philosopher's preference for air rather than water is – or should
be – of less interest to us than his teaching that air should be accorded
the prerogatives of life and divinity. Anaximenes stated: 'Air is God'[5]
and in the fragment quoted above he used the Greek word *pneuma*,
which means much more than air, precisely in order to show that the
whole of nature is permeated by the same breath.

Like his predecessors, Anaximenes spent most of his time observ-
ing natural phenomena and studying astronomy. Let's try to imagine
ourselves attending one of his celebrated lectures.

It is midnight on 7 July 526 BC. The citizens of Miletus have been
in their beds for three hours or more. Anaximenes has summoned us,
together with all those who, as he says, 'thirst after celestial things', to
meet him here on the hill of Kalabak. A moonless night has been
chosen deliberately so that the sky can be best observed.

The sea is a still, black presence. Inhaling deeply we can smell the
flowers in the gardens of Samos, their scent wafted up here on the sea
breeze. The scene is lit by resin torches held by two youths who stand
one on each side of the teacher. The flickering light accentuates the
priestly asceticism of his face. No one dares to break the silence. Now
the aged philosopher moves to the centre of the group and asks for
the torches to be extinguished. It is suddenly very dark and for a while
we can see nothing at all; then, gradually, the darkness becomes

[3]Simplicius, *Comment on the Physics of Aristotle*, 24, 26.
[4]Modern physics has proved the opposite of Anaximenes' theory: the rarefaction
of gases produces a cooling effect, while compression causes a rise in temperature.
[5]Cicero, *De Natura Deorum* I 10, 26.

transparent and the pupils' white tunics emerge in the pale starlight. We look like a convocation of ghosts.

Anaximenes turns his face towards the heavens, then towards us, and now he begins to speak gently, unemotionally, as if he were speaking in the temple.

'My young friends, I am old now and can see the stars more with the eye of memory than with the eyes in my head. You, however, who walk with the Delphic Apollo at your side, can use the sharpness of your eyes to fill your soul with the beauty of the skies. I too, as a boy, came up here to listen to the great Thales, and that was when I heard him say that even among the stars it is possible to find the path which leads to self-knowledge.'

'But was not Chilon, son of Damagetes, the first to say "Know thyself"?'

The speaker is a boy with curly hair, one of the youngest present. The others are taken aback: as Greeks they have been well schooled in *aidos*, respect for their elders, and it is a rare occurrence indeed for a pupil to interrupt the teacher in the middle of a discourse.

Slowly, Anaximenes turns towards the youth and with scarcely a hint of annoyance in his voice replies:

'Thales, the son of Examyes, was the first to say "Know thyself", and it was for this that he was rewarded, by unanimous consent, with the golden tripod. Chilon of Sparta, greedy for fame, tried to steal the maxim from him, that is all; which prompts one to think that there are times when even wisdom would drink from the fountain of Dionysus. However, let us now return to the purpose of our meeting.'

The philosopher pauses once more, as if making a silent appeal for attention, and then begins to speak again in the same quiet tone as before. 'Above us stands the vault of the sky, which covers the earth like a *pileos*, the woollen cap worn by sailors to keep their heads warm when they venture on the sea by night; and, like a *pileos*, which revolves around its wearer's head, the sky revolves about us.[6] The earth is flat, like a table, and round; it is a thin disc

[6]Hippolytus, *Refutation of all Heresies* I 7, 1–8.

borne upon the air, suspended in the middle of the universe; it does not divide the air but covers it like a lid. . .'[7]

'Forgive me, Anaximenes,' the curly-haired boy interrupts once more, 'but you say that the earth covers the air like a lid, yet there is also air above the earth – even though we might not think so because we can neither see it nor touch it like we can see and touch your tunic.'

'Who are you, child?' asks Anaximenes.

'My name is Hecataeus, son of Melantos.'

'So, Hecataeus, I shall reply to your question. Air is above us, beneath us, inside us. You cannot see it because air is only made visible with the help of heat and cold, dryness and moisture. Sometimes it is illuminated by lightning, which is caused by winds cutting through the clouds and producing flashes like oars when they divide the water.[8] Sometimes it takes on the colours of the rainbow, and this occurs after storms when the sun's rays fall on thick condensed air.[9] All that you see is air, and all that you do not see. Even Hecataeus is air.'

'I see,' the boy replies. 'Hecataeus is all air and so is Anaximenes. But speak to us now about the sun and the moon.'

'The sun is a round disc which flames in the sky because its swift movement has made the outer layers incandescent.[10] But mark this: the sun wheels around the earth laterally, never beneath it. . .'

'Then why does it disappear at night?' asks Hecataeus, who now has no inhibitions at all about addressing the master.

'Because at night its path takes it beyond the land of the Thracians and the Odrysae, where gigantic mountains of ice conceal it completely[11] until it reappears in renewed splendour above the green plains of Nineveh and Babylon and sheds its rays upon the two rivers.[12] It is then still too low for us to see, but not for the moon, which takes its light from the sun and floats in the sky like a painted

[7]Aristotle, *De Caelo* II 294b 13–21.
[8]Aetios, II 5, 10.
[9]Aratus of Soli, *Phaenomena*, 455, 1.
[10]Pseudo-Plutarch, *Stromateis* 3.
[11]Hippolytus, *op. cit.* I 7, 1–8.
[12]The Tigris and the Euphrates.

disc.[13] If the fiery orb of the sun were to rotate beneath the earth, as my friend and master Anaximander maintained, we would see the moon disappear every night, piece by piece, like a flower from which a nervous girl plucks the petals one by one.'

'And the stars?'

'Some of these float on the air like fiery leaves; they were produced by moisture rising from the earth and became luminous by rarefaction;[14] these we call 'planets'. The others, far more numerous, are fixed like nails[15] in the vault of the heavens which, as the Chaldeans were the first to observe, is a crystalline hemisphere covered with ice.[16] But now, my young friends, the lesson is over. Return to Miletus and may sleep reward your desire for knowledge.'

The torches are relighted and we begin our descent towards the city. As we walk, everyone joins in a spirited discussion of the master's words. If I understood him aright, Anaximenes maintains that the universe is like one of those glass balls you see in souvenir shops, the kind that fill with flying snow when you turn them upside down; and inside this glass ball the flat disc of the earth is wedged in such a way that it divides the globe into two equal hemispheres of which the lower is filled with air and the upper contains the sun, the moon and all the heavenly bodies. Absorbed in discussing all this with the other pupils, I suddenly notice that the path has become steeper and more dangerous. It is dark and the torches can only light the way for a few. I wonder where the moon has got to, behind which mountain it is hiding now. I should like to ask Anaximenes but cannot summon up the courage. The philosopher is silent: he too is concentrating on the problem of where to place his feet, and from time to time grasps the arm of Hecataeus, who is walking beside him.

[13]Theon of Smyrna, *Elements of Astronomy*, p. 199, 1–2 Hiller.
[14]Hippolytus, *op. cit.* I 7, 1–8.
[15]Aetios, II 14, 3.
[16]P. Tannery, *Pour l'histoire de la science hellène. De Thalès à Empédocle*, Paris 1930, 2nd ed., p. 154.

VI

Peppino

After Thales, Anaximander and Anaximenes, we come to Peppino Russo of Naples (AD 1921–75). Russo, in my considered opinion, has every right to be called the last of the Milesian philosophers and I foresee no difficulty about proving this even though I am well aware that my inclusion of a thinker called Peppino among the Greek philosophers will be dubbed a provocation by some. Let us look at the facts.

Thales said that all things are full of Gods, Anaximander was convinced that the elements were divinities engaged in a constant struggle amongst themselves, and Anaximenes taught that even stones have a soul; so when Peppino Russo asserted that everything in the world has a soul, acquired from humans in the course of its existence, he was only following in the footsteps of the earlier Sages. I could now start expatiating on hylozoism and pantheistic immanentism, but I fear that my reader would take fright and sheer away from any further study of philosophy, so I shall refrain, only remarking that among the ancient philosophers there were several who liked to believe that things possessed souls.[1] We call this way of thinking 'hylozoism' from

[1]Among the philosophers who could be called hylozoists one might mention the Stoics, to whom fire was the animating principle, Straton of Lampsacus, Telesio, Giordano Bruno, Campanella and, most important of all, Spinoza, who attributed various degrees of animation to material objects.

the Greek words *hulè* meaning 'matter' and *zoè* meaning 'life'.

My first encounter with Peppino Russo came about by the purest chance, in 1970, when Don Peppino was living in a little house on the outskirts of Rome in the Vigna Stelluti area. One day I decided to dodge the congested traffic of the Cassia and turned into a side street where, after a couple of bends and when I was least expecting it, I was confronted by an amazing sight: for about a hundred metres, every tree lining the road was laden with dolls and old toys. In spite of the fact that I really had no time to spare, I stopped the car to question the only passer-by who happened to be visible. I was unlucky: the man expressed an immediate impatience with my question, saying that he was sick and tired of the whole thing, that the person responsible for the unsightly mess was *er bambolaro*, the doll-man, and I was wasting my time if I hung around for him because he spent every day raking around rubbish dumps in search of old toys.

I drove down the 'road of the dolls' several times over the next few days without ever catching a glimpse of this famous *bambolaro*, but, in the process, the sight became ever more familiar. By day it looked like Christmas, by night a Dario Argento film. Incidentally, I forgot to mention that *er bambolaro* had hung large placards from the trees, each bearing a different legend – rather like the Sages in Delphi. I'll try to recall some: 'Man, you are Nature, and by destroying Nature you destroy yourself'; 'Last night the world frightened me'; and 'For all your greatness you cannot banish war.'

At last, one day I saw a man pop out from behind a hedge clasping an almost bald teddy bear. I drew up.

'Good morning,' I said, without getting out of the car.

'Good morning,' he replied.

'Forgive me, but I was just wondering why . . . that is, may I ask you, without appearing too inquisitive, why you. . .'

'. . . hang dolls on trees?' Don Peppino rescued me from the embarrassment of a direct question.

'Well, you know how it is, at times one's curiosity. . .'

'Have they already told you that I'm mad?'

'Not exactly,' I replied diplomatically, 'though a fellow I met did give me the impression that you weren't quite his type.'

'Do you believe in the existence of the soul?'

'Naturally!' I exclaimed. 'That is, I suppose so ... I mean ... well, by and large, yes.'

'You don't sound altogether convinced.'

'Oh, I am, I am.'

'So, permit me to say that I think my conviction is rather stronger than yours,' he said, laughing. Then he became suddenly serious again and looked at me narrowly as if to assess what manner of man he was dealing with. 'I'll tell you what: park your car in that space over there and come in for a cup of coffee.'

In the event he offered me bread, cheese and beans, which rather put me in mind of the frugal habits of Epicurus, and between mouthfuls of white wine and slices of pecorino told me all about his life and his theory of the soul.

Don Peppino had served in the Air Force (as a flight-sergeant if I remember rightly), he could play the violin and, in his spare moments, liked to paint. Like all the Milesian philosophers, he had travelled extensively: he had been to America, Australia, France and – significantly in the present context – Rhodes, where, having arrived as a prisoner of war in 1942, he chose to stay and work for nine years. For those who may have forgotten their geography, the island of Rhodes is only a few kilometres south of Miletus. Life is full of strange coincidences!

'So, Don Peppì, you were saying that in your opinion every doll has a soul.'

'Not so fast, my friend, that's not precisely what I said,' admonished my philosopher, slicing pecorino with a kind of jack-knife. 'It's not that all toys, as soon as they leave the factory, automatically have a soul. Not at all. When they are just made they are only things, objects without individuality. But when a child begins to love them, *then*, and only then, does a part of the child's soul enter into the material and bring it to life. From that moment, no matter how broken or scruffy they may have got in the process, toys cannot be thrown away; that is why I go around collecting them from here, there and everywhere and hang them up in the trees, where they can go on living among the leaves and blossoms, come rain, come shine.'

'And I suppose that what applies to dolls would apply equally to any other kind of object?'

'That's only logical. The main thing is to have a clear idea of what we mean by "life" and "death". Let me ask you a very personal question. Have you ever seen the dead body of someone you loved?' Don Peppino paused for a few seconds for my reply, then drew his chair closer to mine and continued in a lower voice. 'It happened to me when my father died. I had always assumed that on the day he died I should be prostrated with grief, but, incredible as this may sound, when it actually happened I felt nothing, I couldn't even shed a tear. I stood there like a ninny, not uttering a word, and I kept racking my brain for excuses. I can't cry, I thought, because I'm too numb, too confused. But I was wrong. The real explanation was much simpler: I refused to recognize the body! That corpse lying there on the deathbed was only a thing, a clearly inanimate object that had nothing whatsoever to do with my father.'

He stopped short, jumped up and left the room, returning in a matter of seconds carrying a pair of spectacles, a stationmaster's watch with a scratched glass, a pocket address book, a pipe and a marble paperweight in the shape of a lion.

'It was not until the day after he died, when I went into his room to find some papers, that I saw a few of those objects which we call 'personal effects'. As soon as I clapped eyes on them, the floodgates of emotion opened and I was able to weep. That was where my father had hidden himself: in the tartan rug, in the gold-topped fountain pen, in the leather armchair with its scuffed armrests, in the hundred and one objects with which he had shared his lonely existence day by day.'

I longed to make some suitable comment but none came to mind. Apart from anything else, the sight of that motley collection had inspired in me a strange sense of unease, as if Don Peppino's father were actually present. Finally, just to break the silence, I asked another question.

'And this knife, does it, too, have a soul?'

'Without a doubt,' he answered unhesitatingly, picking up the knife by the blade and waving it in front of my face. 'This is a piece of my soul and, I may add, of my personality too. Now, in the hands of a peace-loving person, this knife has become a simple domestic utensil, devoid of any aggressive connotation, only good for slicing cheese. But this room has a soul of its own, too, and the neighbourhood and the city as a whole. The souls of these last two are complex, shaped by the influence of successive generations.'

'Do you mean it's a sort of common denominator of the souls of all those who have lived in a certain place?'

'Not quite. The soul of any city is individual in its own right, a presence formed gradually by the passage of time and by all the people who have lived there and experienced their joys and sorrows there over the centuries. The older a city is, the less its soul can be altered by the latest generation. Take Rome, for example: for hundreds of years it was the gathering place of all those who had anything to say. Michelangelo, Caravaggio, Bernini, Horace, Giordano Bruno and thousands of other artists and thinkers came here to live and to die. How could the stones of Rome ever be the same as those of Los Angeles?! I'm certain that if I were to be kidnapped, blindfolded and then released in some street in Milan or Bologna that was completely unknown to me, as soon as I was freed I would know which city I was in. I would say at once: "This is Milan" or "This is Bologna". Someone might ask me how I could tell, had I perhaps caught a glimpse of the Duomo or the Asinelli Tower? Not at all, I would reply, but my skin has sensed the spirit of the air, of the roofs, of the plasterwork of the city.'

As no coffee had yet appeared, I decided to go and make it myself. Don Peppino was too absorbed in his train of thought to think of such mundane matters: he just passed me the things I needed.

'It follows that even this kitchen has a soul, and not derived only from me, obviously. I often wonder who lived in this house in years gone by. A peasant? A tailor? A murderer? Only one's heart can give an answer.'

I looked around me and had the impression that I was being watched by a thousand eyes as I prepared the coffee.

VII
Pythagoras Superstar

When Hermes[1] wanted to give his son Aethalides a present and told him he could choose any gift he liked except immortality, Aethalides wisely asked for an eternal memory so that he might retain, even through death, the experiences of the present and all subsequent lives. Thanks to this faculty, Pythagoras claimed to have already lived four times:[2] first as Hermes' son Aethalides, then as Euphorbus, a warrior wounded at Troy by Menelaus, then Hermotimus, during which reincarnation he gave proof of the previous one by recognizing the shield of Menelaus, and finally as Pyrrhus, a poor fisherman of Delos. Between one rebirth and another, his soul had migrated into several species of animals and even into a few plants, and had also visited Hades[3] where he saw Homer hanging from a tree and Hesiod chained to a column, both having been guilty of treating the Gods with disrespect. Nor did the reappearances of Pythagoras end with the philosopher's death. Several later historians[4] say that he was reincarnated as a certain Periander, then as a man called (again) Aethalides and finally in the perfumed robes of a beautiful woman who was, by profession, a whore. By calculating the intervals between these reincarnations we arrive at a cycle of 216 years,[5] so a reappearance should have been due in about AD 1810.

[1]According to some sources, Apollo was the father of Aethalides.
[2]Diogenes Laertius, *op. cit.* VIII 4.
[3]Diogenes Laertius, *op. cit.* VIII 21.
[4]Aulus Gellius, *Noctes Atticae* IV 11, 14.
[5]216 was one of the Pythagorean magic numbers, being 6^3.

Taking his political views into account, he may even have been reborn as Count Cavour, whose birth did occur in that year.

Herodotus tells us that Pythagoras had a slave called Zalmoxis who was a God.[6] Once freed and having become very rich, he built himself a magnificent house and invited the *crème de la crème* of his native town to a banquet. During the feast he informed his guests that they would never die and that he himself was a God who came and went from Hades whenever he wished. He then disappeared into an underground room that he had thoughtfully provided for the purpose and remained there for three years until, long after everyone thought he was dead, he re-emerged, as sprightly as ever, and was venerated as a God by the Getae.

Such stories tell us immediately that imagination has had a field-day where the life of Pythagoras is concerned. Serious historians have always quite rightly refused to have anything to do with the anecdotes. For myself, seriousness comes hard and I have no hesitation whatsoever about retelling anything I have read, especially the things that have amused me most.

I only hope that one day somebody will write a eulogy in praise of the Lie, for the Lie, whatever people say, has a place in history. If Iamblichus and Porphyry, Pythagoras' principal historians, thought it worth their while to write about certain episodes in the life of the philosopher, one may assume that these episodes are at least in character and therefore help in a general understanding of the personality. And even if Truth were eventually to prove that some of these anecdotes were false, Truth would be the loser, for she would have admitted her own inferiority to fiction!

Pythagoras, son of a jeweller called Mnesarchus, was born in 570 BC on the island of Samos, not far from the city of Miletus. Thanks to a letter of introduction from his uncle Zoïlus,[7] he was educated by the great Pherecydes from whom the first thing he learnt, according to Appollonius,[8] was to perform miracles. When Pherecydes died he decided to pursue his studies in the mathematical sciences with the

[6]Herodotus, *The Histories* IV 95.
[7]Diogenes Laertius, *op. cit.* VIII 2.
[8]Diogenes Laertius, *loc. cit.*

most illustrious teachers of his time, the Egyptian priests. So he packed three silver flagons from his father's shop and a letter of recommendation from the tyrant Polycrates to the Pharoah Amasis in his suitcase and boarded the first available ship. As you may have noticed, even at that time the wheels were oiled with backhanders and recommendations! Nevertheless, as soon as he arrived in Egypt his plans received a setback: despite the silver flagons and the fact that he was the Pharoah's *protégé*, the priests of Heliopolis hypocritically declared themselves unworthy of so illustrious a pupil and packed him off to the older and more venerable priests in Memphis; these in their turn off-loaded him on to the terrible priests of Thebes (sometimes called Diospolis the Great) who, finding themselves at the end of the line with nowhere else to throw the hot potato, put him through a series of the most rigorous trials. They had calculated without the stubborn character of Pythagoras. The philosopher overcame every obstacle brilliantly and in the end won the admiration of his persecutors who now had no option but to welcome him as a brother and initiate him into all their mysteries.[9]

Having learnt all he could from the Egyptians, Pythagoras continued his education with further travels;[10] various historians assert that he learnt astronomy from the Chaldeans, logistics and geometry from the Phoenicians and occult lore from the Magi.[11] His encounters with contemporary personalities are as numerous as they are improbable. I have even read one account of a visit to Numa Pompilius who, unless I am much mistaken, died a hundred years before Pythagoras' birth. Among the more significant encounters we should mention that with the Persian Zarathustra,[12] from whom Pythagoras learnt the theory of dualism. Everything, according to Zarathustra, is generated by the opposition of Good and Evil; man and light he ranged on the side of the former, darkness and woman on the side of the latter. It is indeed strange, but none of the great spiritual teachers – Zarathustra, Isaiah, Confucius, Muhammad, St Paul et cetera et

[9]Porphyry, *Life of Pythagoras* 7.
[10]Porphyry, *op. cit.* 6.
[11]The Magi were one of the six tribes of Asia Minor; they were famous as exponents of magic, the word deriving from this connection.
[12]Hippolytos, *Confutation of all Heresies*, I 2, 12.

cetera – has ever placed woman on the side of the angels. One wonders why.

But to return to Pythagoras; once his studies were ended he went back to his homeland and became a tutor to the son of Polycrates, the tyrant of Samos. And here we should, perhaps, pause for a brief word on Polycrates, the 'old ruffian'[13] of the sixth century. He was not so much a king as a dyed-in-the-wool pirate whose ships raided all who dared approach the Ionian coast. His foreign policy consisted of invariably allying himself with the lowest of the low unless he caught wind of a change of fortunes, when he changed sides accordingly. He was a ne'er-do-well, and as for his behaviour at court, he did nothing but indulge in riotous living in the company of intellectuals such as Ibycus and the poet Anacreon plus a hundred or so beautiful girls and pretty young men.[14] For Pythagoras, a moralist like all the great teachers, this self-indulgent life held no appeal and he decided, despite his forty years or more, to take ship once more and sail to Croton on the Italian coast.[15] Here the assembly of the elders invited him to teach the wisdom of the Greeks to their young people and he naturally leapt at the chance to organize a class of some three hundred students and thus provide himself with a formidable power-base.

Pythagoras founded a school, perhaps better described as a religious sect, whose members were obliged to adhere very strictly to a series of extraordinary rules. Here are some of them.

1 To abstain from beans.
2 Not to break bread.
3 Not to stir the fire with iron.
4 Not to touch a white cock.
5 Not to eat the heart.
6 Not to look in a mirror beside a light.
7 Not to leave the impress of your body upon the bedclothes when you rise.
8 To stir the ashes when you remove the pot from the fire.

[13]Bertrand Russell, *History of Western Philosophy* (2nd ed. London, 1961) pp. 49–50.
[14]Herodotus, *op. cit.* III 39–46, 121.
[15]Diogenes Laertius, *op. cit.* VIII 3.

Perhaps we should try in vain to understand anything of this. Religious precepts are often no more than a discipline imposed to inspire solidarity within the group. In this case, the most we can do is extract some metaphorical meaning. The injunction not to break bread could be interpreted as 'do not loosen the ties of friendship', and 'do not stir the fire with iron' might mean 'be prepared to forgive'. Whatever we make of the rest, the strangest of the commands of Pythagoras remains that concerning beans.[16] Heaven only knows why Pythagoras should have hated that innocuous vegetable as he did! Aristotle suggested the reason might lie in the resemblance of the bean to testicles; according to others, however, the philosopher suffered from an allergy that had plagued him from childhood. All we know for certain is that beans could not even be mentioned in his presence.

Once initiated, members of the sect lived together in a community holding all things in common. Every evening at sunset they were required to ask themselves three questions: (a) What evil have I done? (b) What good have I done? (c) What have I omitted to do? Then they had to speak the following sentence: 'I swear by Him who has revealed to our soul the divine *tetraktys*.'[17]

The Master taught every evening; people flocked from all over the world to hear him, but he allowed none to see him, speaking from behind a curtain. Those who managed to catch a glimpse of him, no matter how fleeting, congratulated themselves upon their good fortune for the rest of their lives.[18] 'With his distinguished countenance, wavy locks and white robe, he would make his appearance, a man altogether majestic in bearing.'[19] He began every lesson with the words: 'I swear by the air that I breathe and the water that I drink that I will never suffer censure on account of that which I am about to say.'[20] Which gives us some insight into Pythagoras' attitudes to democracy.

[16]Aulus Gellius, *op. cit.* IV 11, 1–2.
[17]The 'divine' *tetraktys* (see p. 45) was a configuration of the number 10, which the Pythagoreans revered as a divine revelation.
[18]Diogenes Laertius, *op. cit.* VIII 15.
[19]J. Burckhardt, *op. cit.* p. 286.
[20]Diogenes Laertius, *op. cit.* VIII 6.

Only a few fortunate people were ever admitted into his presence, even his pupils being denied the privilege until they had completed five years of study. One of these 'novices' did once manage to infiltrate his private apartments, however, and having caught sight of him taking a bath in a tub was able to report back to the others that he had a golden thigh.[21] Aelian reports, however, that it was Pythagoras himself who showed his golden thigh in the theatre at Olympia.[22]

Pythagoras was wont to divide his followers into two categories: mathematicians, those who had rightful access to knowledge (*mathemata*), and akousmatics, whose only duty was to obey the rules. To preserve the purity of the nucleic sect, he invented a secret language for the exclusive use of its members, consisting of numerical codes, symbolic messages and a variety of cunning devices all calculated to protect the power-base by controlling information. In practical terms Pythagoras could be considered the inventor of freemasonry, or at least his sect was the precursor of all later secret societies. The sect had all the characteristics of a masonic lodge: secrecy, initiation rites, a Grand Master, fraternal cooperation, secret symbols, compasses, set squares and so on. With regard to secrecy, no quarter was shown to those who transgressed. One student, Hippasus, revealed to the world the existence of irrational numbers, a discovery which threatened the whole theory of numerical harmony upon which the Pythagorean system was based. The traitor did not get very far: cursed by the Master, he made a desperate bid to escape and was drowned only a few miles off Croton.

Many miraculous feats were attributed to Pythagoras, of which I shall list only some of the least incredible. He killed a deadly snake by biting it.[23] He held conversations with a bear over a period of many years.[24] He persuaded a heifer to refrain from eating beans.[25] He caressed a white eagle who came down from the sky just to greet him.[26] He was seen at one and the same time in Croton and at

[21]Diogenes Laertius, *op. cit.* VIII 11.
[22]Aelian (Claudius Aelianus), *Various History* II 26.
[23]Iamblichus, *Life of Pythagoras* 142.
[24]Aelian, *op. cit.* IV 17.
[25]Iamblichos, *op. cit.* 60–1, 142.
[26]Aelian, *op. cit.* IV 17.

Metapontium.[27] As he was crossing the Nessos, the river god addressed him with the words: 'Greetings, O Pythagoras'.[28,29]

The supernatural character of Pythagoras was enhanced by the attitude of his students, who considered him almost a demigod. They were wont to say: 'There are in the universe men and gods and beings like Pythagoras.'[30] His name was never mentioned explicitly in conversation but he was referred to obliquely as 'that Man' or, more dogmatically, *autos efè* (he himself said), which, translated into the Latin *ipse dixit*, closed every kind of argument for many a century.

The rules, the mysteries and the dogmatic nature of his teaching eventually wore down the patience of the more democratically minded among the Crotonians. As we say in Naples, *Dalle e dalle se scassano pure 'e metalle!* – which is roughly equivalent to Ovid's 'Dripping water hollows out a stone'. It has to be admitted that the Pythagoreans gave their neighbours little enough cause to love them. They looked down their noses at everybody else, they would only shake hands with one of their own number and they tried to impose their beliefs upon everyone. Now, almost anything may be forgiven great men apart from an attempt to reform others at any cost. And it was mainly due to the collective bigotry of the Pythagoreans that the Crotonians decided to declare war upon the Sybarites who were, according to Pythagoras, guilty of a carefree, thoughtless way of life. The outcome (typical of victories achieved under the banner of religious reform) was that elegant, sophisticated Sybaris was razed to the ground and its inhabitants put to the sword.[31]

Meanwhile, there was an anti-Pythagorean faction forming in Croton. The head of this opposition was a certain Chilon, a young man of high birth and violent nature who, having been refused admittance to the Pythagorean sect, had vowed to be revenged upon them.[32] One night he organized a gang of hooligans to surround the Pythagoreans'

[27]Aelian, *op. cit.* II 26.
[28]Iamblichus, *op. cit.* 134.
[29]Please note that I have not referred to Pythagoras as the discoverer of X-rays and Pythagorean orangeade as did Francesco Grillo in his *Life of Pythagoras*.
[30]Iamblichus, *op. cit.* 31.
[31]Diodorus Siculus, *Biblioteca Historica*, XII 9, 2–10, 1.
[32]Iamblichus, *op. cit.* 248–9.

headquarters in the villa belonging to an athlete, Milo, and having summoned the philosopher in vain to come out, set fire to the house. Only a few managed to escape, including Archippus, Lysis and Pythagoras himself, but unfortunately there was a large field of beans behind the house, and rather than cross it the aged philosopher chose to stand and meet his death at the hands of the conspirators. Porphyry's version is different, however:[33] he says that Chilon's men were nice chaps, and having caught Pythagoras they then released him saying: 'Dear Pythagoras, you have a great brain but we like our own laws and we don't want you to try to change them. Be off with you and leave us in peace!' Finally, Dikaearchos tells us[34] that the philosopher fled to Metapontium and took refuge in the temple of the Muses where, saying that he had no wish to live any longer, he starved himself to death. Some sources say that he died at the age of 70, others 90, 107 or even 150 plus.[35]

When Leon the tyrant of Phlius asked him who he was, Pythagoras replied, 'a philosopher',[36] and that was the first time that the word, which means literally 'lover of wisdom', had ever been pronounced. But in spite of his being the first philosopher in history to claim the title, Pythagoras' taste for power soon made the school he had founded more of a political sect than a university for the study of philosophy. There is a theory that Pythagoreanism may have been a branch of Orphism, a religious movement very popular in seventh-century Greece whose adepts, with the excuse of identifying themselves with the god Dionysus, spent their time most enjoyably in orgies and Bacchanals. Well now, in spite of my suspicions about the personality of Pythagoras, this is something I refuse to believe. To identify the Pythagoreans with the followers of the Orphic religion is rather like confusing the saffron-robed Hari Krishnans with the Italian football fans an hour after a World Cup victory over Brazil: the first group is as contemplative as the second is Dionysiac. And quite apart from his discoveries in mathematics, Pythagoras was distinguished by a vastly

[33]Porphyry, *op. cit.* 56.
[34]Dikaearchos, fr. 34 Wehrli.
[35]Iamblichus, *op. cit.* 265.
[36]Diogenes Laertius, *op. cit.* III 8.

superior intelligence and his continuous attempts to unite reason and mysticism.

Pythagoras never wrote a book, so for our knowledge of his teaching we have to rely on the accounts of the writers among his followers such as Alcmaeon, his personal physician, Archytas, the ruler of Taras, and Philolaus, a young Crotonian. Aristotle also refers to him here and there, but, between ourselves, always with a certain coolness as if he regarded Pythagoras as slightly non-U. He mentions him by name only five times and gets round the problem on other occasions by using phrases like 'Those who are called Pythagoreans say. . .'

Such is the welter of information that we have about Pythagoras, that in order to illustrate his teaching without getting bogged down it seems sensible to concentrate upon three of his fundamental doctrines: transmigration of the soul (or metempsychosis), theory of numbers and cosmology.

We have already mentioned his theory of the transmigration of souls at the beginning of this chapter when we reported Pythagoras' claim to have lived in no less than four previous epochs and to have 'visited', in the intervals between one reincarnation and the next, the bodies of various animals and even plants. This idea he almost certainly imported from the Far East, where there are still people today who hold such beliefs. According to the theory of metempsychosis, the soul passes from one body into another and is either promoted to a superior state (merchant, athlete, spectator)[37] or relegated to an inferior one (tree, dog, sheep, pig, etc.) according to the person's behaviour in this life. Death, according to Alcmaeon,[38] is the link between an 'end' and a 'beginning', so that although the body dies, the soul, which is immortal, describes a circular trajectory just

---

[37]'In this life – Pythagoras said – there are three kinds of men, just as there are three sorts of people who come to the Olympic Games. The lowest class is made up of those who come to buy and sell, the next above them are those who compete. Best of all, however, are those who come simply to look on. The greatest purification of all is, therefore, disinterested science, and it is the man who devotes himself to that, the true philosopher, who has most effectually released himself from the wheel of birth.' Burnet, *Early Greek Philosophy*, p. 98; also quoted *in toto* by Bertrand Russell in *History of Western Philosophy*. p. 52.

[38]Alcmaeon, fr. 2 Diels-Kranz.

like the stars in the heavens. The body, Philolaus adds, is nothing but a tomb, a prison in which the soul is confined until it has expiated its guilt.[39] Here, then, we have the Pythagorean ethic: Behave, or no promotion!

The theory of metempsychosis led to Pythagoras being widely ridiculed by his contemporaries and lampooned by leading drama-tists. In one of Xenophanes' plays the philosopher is shown in the act of restraining a man he sees beating his dog.[40]

> 'I pray you,' says Pythagoras, 'do not beat your dog, for I fear that the soul of my friend may be within him.'
> 'How can you tell that?' the man asks.
> 'I recognized his voice.'

Not even Shakespeare could resist a dig. The following exchange occurs in *Twelfth Night*:

> CLOWN: What is the opinion of Pythagoras concerning wild fowl?
> MALVOLIO: That the soul of our grandam might haply inhabit a bird.
> CLOWN: What think'st thou of his opinion?
> MALVOLIO: I think nobly of the soul, and no way approve his opinion.
> CLOWN: Fare thee well. Remain thou still in darkness: thou shalt hold th'opinion of Pythagoras ere I will allow of thy wits; and fear to kill a woodcock, lest thou dispossess the soul of thy grandam.

It is not in metempsychosis, however, that we find the essence of Pythagorean thought, but rather in the theory that numbers are the *archè*, the primordial element of the universe. In other words, that which Thales declared to be water and Anaximenes air, Pythagoras identified with number, and I must admit that the theory leaves me somewhat perplexed. It may be possible to imagine a table as made up of a quantity of compressed molecules of water or air, but it is another matter to try to see it as a collection of numbers all squashed together. Pythagoras maintained in fact that numbers have magnitude. In his

[39] Philolaus, fr. 14 Diels-Kranz.
[40] Diogenes Laertius, *op. cit.* VIII 36.

work on the Pythagorean numbers[41] Speusippus categorically states that One is a point (a kind of atom), Two a straight line, Three a plane figure and Four a solid. And he enlarges upon this saying that two units constitute a line, three a plane and four a solid. So, on the basis that everything in the world, including ourselves, has a shape, it must be possible to express this shape as lines and points and therefore, in the final analysis, as numbers. Aristotle tells us that Eurytus, a second-generation Pythagorean and disciple of Philolaus, took it into his head to determine the characteristic number of all sorts of living things, and to this end he set himself to count the number of pebbles required to construct the image of a man and of a horse.[42]

Pythagoras was struck not only by the physical qualities of numbers but also by the fact that all natural phenomena seem to be regulated by a superior logic; in particular, he noticed a constant relation between the length of a lyre string and the main musical intervals (1:2 for the octave, 3:2 for the fifth, 4:3 for the fourth) which impressed him so much that he believed God to be an engineer extraordinary and a mathematical law called Harmony to be in control of the universe.

For the Pythagoreans, wisdom lay in Number, beauty in Harmony. In the beginning, they argued, there had been Chaos (or disorder); then the Monad (the number One) had created the numbers which gave rise to points and lines, and finally Harmony had arrived to determine right relationships between everything. The result was, for Pythagoras, the Cosmos, Order.[43]

Health, virtue, friendship, art and music were all intrinsically manifestations of Harmony. According to Alcmaeon,[44] health was the perfect attunement of heat and cold within the body, virtue the control of the passions, and so on. Even social justice, according to Archytas, was only a matter of harmony. To avoid confusion, we should mention that social justice for the progressives of fifth-century Greece was a rather different animal from that pursued by our own

[41]Speusippus, fr. 4 Lang.
[42]Aristotle, *Metaphysics* XIV 5, 1092b 8.
[43]Diogenes Laertius, *op. cit.* VIII 25.
[44]Alcmaeon, fr. 4 Diels-Kranz.

trade unions today. For Archytas, a good system of social justice could
be arrived at only when each worker was rewarded according to his
merits. In modern terms this makes him an advocate of piece-work,
stipulating high wages for good workers and nothing at all for idlers.

Having mentioned Archytas, I think we should pause for a moment
and take a look at this extraordinary character. Born in Tarentum,
Archytas was at one and the same time a philosopher, a mathematician
and a great statesman. Living as he did towards the end of the fifth
century and into the fourth BC it is, I think, unlikely that he ever met
Pythagoras. However, he undertook a political career in complete
accordance with the ideals of Pythagoreanism and led his city for many
years. We know that he saved the life of his friend Plato when the
philosopher had been condemned to death by Dionysios, tyrant of
Syracuse,[45] that he invented the rattle with the express purpose of
distracting children and preventing them from damaging things of
value,[46] and that, being an enthusiastic aeromodeller, he managed to
construct a wooden dove that actually flew.[47]

But to return to Pythagoras and his passion for mathematics, he
seems to have believed in a kind of pecking-order even among
numbers: there were aristocrats and there were plebians. The number
10 was divine, but 1, 2, 3 and 4 were also held in especial reverence:
their sum equals 10 and together they form the divine triangle, the
tetraktys:

```
            *

         *     *

      *     *     *

   *     *     *     *
```

'Everything that we know possesses a number,' said Philolaus,[48] and
every number has a special significance. If we examine the texts of

[45]Diogenes Laertius, *op. cit.* VII 79.
[46]Aristotle, *Politics* VIII 6, 1340b 27–30.
[47]Aulus Gellius, *op. cit.* X 12, 9.
[48]Philolaus, fr. 4 Diels-Kranz.

Speusippus, Archytas and Philolaus very closely, we can construct a sort of Pythagorean *Smorfia*[49] where 1 represents intelligence, 2 opinion (always two edged), 3 (or, according to Aristotle,[50] 5) marriage, 4 justice, 7 the 'right time' (maybe a reference to the seven-day week) and so on. Numbers could al‿o, according to the Pythagoreans, have therapeutic value, hence the magic squares inscribed on silver discs and worn as a prevention against plague, cholera and venereal diseases, a custom which survived through the Middle Ages and into the Renaissance. It occurs to me that although it might be difficult to persuade airport officials to accept a numeric talisman in lieu of a vaccination certificate, one might experiment with one of the simpler forms:

13	3	2	16
8	10	11	5
12	6	7	9
1	15	14	4

In this figure, by adding up the numbers in any column or any diagonal, the total is invariably 34.[51] The same result is achieved by adding the numbers in each corner, or the four central numbers, or even the numbers contained within each quarter of the diagram.

All these secret correlations, both between numbers and within natural phenomena, must have caused enormous excitement to Pythagoras. So we can imagine the gloom that descended upon him when he discovered the incommensurability of the diagonal and the side of a square. How could this possibly be?! Everything, up to this point, had appeared to obey the laws of Harmony, so how on earth

---

[49]*Translator's note*: In Naples, the name given to the book of dreams from which lottery numbers are chosen. (See *Thus Spake Bellavista*, Chap. XXVI) *Smorfia* is derived from *Morpheus*, the Roman god of sleep.

[50]Aristotle, *Metaphysics* 4 1978b 21.

[51]This figure appears in Albrecht Dürer's famous painting *Melancholy*, where the numbers in the middle of the bottom row, 15 and 14, give the date of the work: 1514.

13	3	2	16
8	10	11	5
12	6	7	9
1	15	14	4

could an insoluble problem like this suddenly rear its head? And to think that he himself had made the discovery that in a right-angled triangle the square on the hypotenuse is equal to the sum of the squares on the other two sides![52] Yet here was that selfsame wretched hypotenuse refusing to allow itself to be divided by one of its sides! The discovery of the so-called irrational numbers was a punch below the belt for the poor Pythagoreans. And to make matters worse, one of his own disciples, the traitor Hippasus, had to go and blabber about it to all and sundry!

To end the chapter on Pythagoras, let's have a look at his cosmology. For the first time in the history of philosophy, we are forced out of our armchair at the centre of the universe and presented instead with a central fire no better defined. The Pythagoreans referred to it as 'the Mother of the Gods'. Fancy. Around this fire revolved ten heavenly bodies: the earth, the moon, the sun, the five planets then known, the fixed stars and, in order to arrive at the magic figure of 10 that seems to have been a bit of an obsession with the Pythagoreans, a heavenly body they called the *Antichthon* or Counter-Earth.[53] This was a planet similar to our own in every way and following the same orbit, but situated diametrically opposite to us, relative to the central fire, and therefore invisible.

According to Pythagoras, the ten heavenly bodies move in circular

[52]Apollodorus said that when Pythagoras discovered his famous theorem, he sacrificed a hundred oxen to the Gods, which, for a man who refused to eat meat because he disliked the killing of animals, is decidedly peculiar. Cf. Diogenes Laertius, *op. cit.* VIII 12.
[53]Aristotle, *De caelo* II 13, 293a 18.

orbits emitting a sweet musical sound, the so-called 'Music of the Spheres'.[54] Unhappily, no one can hear this music because it is continuous and the mortal ear can only discern sounds which contrast with the surrounding silence.[55]

Beyond the ten celestial orbits lies infinite space. Archytas, to prove the existence of the infinite, once asked: 'If I were to sit at the extreme limit of the universe, could I or could I not stretch out my hand? If I could, it means that beyond this limit there is yet more space.'[56]

[54]Simplicius, *op. cit.* 732, 26.
[55]Aristotle, *De caelo* II 9, 290b 12.
[56]Simplicius, *op. cit.* 467, 26.

VIII
Heraclitus the Obscure

Heraclitus was born in Ephesus, on the Ionian coast, a few kilometres north of Kusadasi where there is now a splendid Club Méditerranée holiday village. The frenetic liveliness of the village with its tireless GOs,[1] windsurfers streaking across the water and bonfires on the beach, chimes in rather well with the philosophy of Becoming. The sociability required of the customers is, however, slightly less Heraclitean, since the philosopher was an out-and-out aristocrat and consequently never socialized with anyone.

Heraclitus' date of birth is very uncertain. Some put it at 540 BC, others as late as the beginning of the next century. This lack of precise information is due to the fact that ancient historians attached little importance to the date on which an eminent man happened to be born and referred instead to the years of his prime, the so-called *akmè*. And they used a particularly apt verb for this: to 'flourish'. Heraclitus 'flourished' during the 69th Olympiad (around 500 BC).[2]

His father, Bloson or Blyson, was a direct descendant of the founder of the colony, Androcles, who in turn was the son of Codrus, tyrant of Athens.[3] By virtue of this royal descent, his family held an hereditary right to the title of *Basileus*, the highest priestly office in the *polis*. This very elevated niche in society would have reverted automatically to Heraclitus as the firstborn son had he not, when the time came,

---

[1]*Translator's note: Gentils Organisateurs.*
[2]Diogenes Laertius, *op. cit.* IX 1.
[3]Strabo, XIV 632–33.

renounced it in favour of his brother. I relate these details because it seems to me that Heraclitus' morose, irascible character provides us with a key to his mind. He was an aristocrat and an intellectual – which is the same as saying an arch-snob – and despised his fellow men, particularly the ignorant and the superstitious. Here are a couple of the fragments attributed to him:[4]

- ... there are many bad and few good [men] ... for most of them are glutted like beasts.[5]
- Men are as unable to understand [my teaching] when they hear it for the first time as before they have heard it at all ... and know not what they are doing when awake, even as they forget what they do in sleep.[6]

He boasted that he had never had a teacher, and when he needed to discuss anything, he would say: 'Wait a moment while I go and inquire of myself.'[7] The only sage he esteemed among his predecessors was old Bias ('most men are bad', *see* Chapter I). For the rest he had nothing but scorn. 'The learning of many things teacheth not understanding, else would it have taught Hesiod and Pythagoras, Xenophanes and Hecataeus.'[8]

Having renounced his position in favour of his brother, he went to play knuckle-bones with some boys at the temple of Artemis, and when the Ephesians remonstrated with him, he answered: 'O rascals, why are you astonished? Is it not better to play games with children than to take part with you in the government of this city?'[9] Despite his extremely elevated opinion of himself, he had no political ambitions whatsoever. The Persian king Darius, who loved to surround himself with intellectuals, once wrote him a long letter inviting him to his court where, one gathers, he would have been showered with gold. But once again

[4]*Translator's note*: The author's numbering of the fragments according to Colli has been replaced by that found in *Historia Philosophiae Graecae*, H. Ritter et L. Preller, ed. Wellmann, Gotha, 1898, as quoted by Burnet in *Early Greek Philosophy*, p. 132ff.

[5]R. P. 31a.

[6]R. P. 32.

[7]Diogenes Laertius, *op. cit.* IX 5.

[8]R. P. 31.

[9]Diogenes Laertius, *op. cit.* IX 3.

our philosopher turned down a 'safe job' and told Darius that he had a horror of the insolent thirst for popularity that bred nothing but envy and wickedness.[10] That was completely in character. His fellow citizens, on the other hand, were of a different mettle: the prevailing moral climate in Ephesus was one of carefree enjoyment and letting the future take care of itself. Historians tell us that when the city was being besieged by the Persians, the citizens continued to behave as if their stocks of food were inexhaustible; when, due to the length of the siege, these stocks did begin to run low, 'one by the name of Heraclitus intervened at an assembly of the people and, without saying a word, took a handful of crushed barley, mixed it with water and began to eat it, sitting on the floor in their midst.'[11] The citizens understood the mute reproof and immediately started to tighten their belts, and the Persians, discouraged, eventually gave up and went home. Maybe we could solve other economic crises with an equally simple gesture by asking a man known for his wisdom to eat, let's say, a portion of fish and chips in front of the television cameras, so that the viewers, impressed by such frugality, would realize that fillet steak is not the only option!

Because he despised the common herd,[12] Heraclitus ranged himself politically on the side of the tyrants. He said, 'It is also law to obey the counsel of one.'[13] To be fair, I should explain that the reigning tyrant in Ephesus at the time was Hermodorus, a man of exceptional virtue and an old friend of the philosopher's family. We can imagine how it must have infuriated Heraclitus when the Ephesians banished Hermodorus with the following explanation: 'We will have none who is worthiest among us; or if there be any such, let him go elsewhere and consort with others.'[14] Heraclitus not only remonstrated with the Ephesians but invited them all to hang themselves, man by man, and leave the government of the city to beardless boys. He then abandoned the city and became a hermit.

The final period of his life was the hardest; he was reduced to living

[10]Diogenes Laertius, *op. cit.* IX 14.
[11]Plutarch, *De garrulitate* (*Moralia*) 17, 511 B.
[12]Diogenes Laertius, *op. cit.* IX 6.
[13]R. P. 49a.
[14]Diogenes Laertius, *op. cit.* IX 2.

like an animal, eating only grass and herbs. He wrote a book, *On Nature*, which, to save it from falling into the wrong hands, he deposited in the temple of Artemis.[15] The writings contained in this work were promptly declared by all and sundry to be completely incomprehensible and their author went down in history as 'Heraclitus the Obscure' (*ho skoteinós*).[16]

Socrates was one of the first to see the book. He commented: 'The part I understand is excellent, and so, I dare say, is the part I do not understand; but it needs a Delian diver to get to the bottom of it.'[17] In other words, only a deep-sea diver, used to the darkness of the watery depths, would have a chance of making anything of it. For his part, Aristotle complained about the dreadful punctuation and the disjointedness of the phrases.

The truth of the matter was, of course, that the ageing and, let's admit it, cantankerous philosopher had no desire to be understood. His style was deliberately oracular, and the oracle, as he himself remarked, 'neither utters nor hides his meaning, but shows it by a sign'.[18] He had absolutely no interest in communicating with the masses, having dismissed them as 'fools [who] when they hear are like the deaf: of them does the saying bear witness they are absent when present.'[19]

At the age of sixty he contracted dropsy; his body became swollen with water and he had to return to the city to seek medical advice. As you might imagine, old Heraclitus had never had a good word for doctors. Among his fragmentary sayings is one where he marvels at 'physicians who cut, burn, stab and torture the sick and then demand a fee for it which they do not deserve to get.'[20] Besides this ingrained antipathy, his natural incommunicativeness had now been increased by years of solitude, so he began to speak in riddles even with his doctors, asking them if they 'were able to transform a flood into a drought'. They

---

[15]Diogenes Laertius, *op. cit.* IX 6.
[16]skoteinós can also be translated as 'dark'; the epithet was applied to Heraclitus both on account of the obscurity of his utterances and in reference to his lonely and melancholy life.
[17]Diogenes Laertius, *op. cit.* II 22.
[18]R. P. 30 a.
[19]R. P. 31 a.
[20]R. P. 47 c.

could make neither head nor tail of this and he cursed the lot of them.

Heraclitus' dropsy was another of the strange quirks of fate to which the philosophers seemed to be prone. For him to be plagued by water was as ironical as Pythagoras' death in a field of beans. To appreciate the irony one has to know that Heraclitus had declared water to be the worst part of human nature. The soul, he said, is composed of 'measures' of fire and water, the proportions varying from individual to individual, but while fire elevates man towards the higher goals, water drags him down to the baser passions. 'A dry soul is the wisest and best,' he says, but 'a man when he gets drunk is led by a beardless lad, tripping, knowing not where he steps, having his soul moist.'[21]

When he fell ill, Heraclitus applied his own remedy: 'He buried himself in a cow shed, expecting that the noxious damp humour would be drawn out of him by the warmth of the manure.'[22] According to Hermippus and Neanthes of Cyzicus, however, he got his servants to plaster him with cow-dung while he lay in the sun, but 'being unrecognizable when so transformed, he was devoured by dogs'.[23]

He was a pessimist. In one of his most dramatic utterances he declared: 'Men wish to live, but even more do they wish to die, and they beget children in order to leave other destinies of death behind them.'[24] This is the Freudian concept of the 'death-wish' making its first-ever appearance in European thought.

The melancholy Heraclitus, as Theophrastus described him,[25] undoubtedly belongs in the category of rationalist philosophers: his scorn for the masses was only second to his scorn for Zeus and the whole company of Olympians. 'The world,' he said, 'no one of gods or men has made.'[26] He openly criticized those who prayed and offered sacrifices, saying: 'To address prayers to images is like talking to a house instead of to those who dwell in it ... They vainly purify themselves by defiling themselves with blood, just as if one who had

[21]R. P. 42.
[22]Diogenes Laertius, *op. cit.* IX 3.
[23]Diogenes Laertius, *op. cit.* IX 4.
[24]Fr. 86 in Bywater's *Heracliti Ephesii reliquiae*, Oxford 1877.
[25]Diogenes Laertius, *op. cit.* IX 6.
[26]R. P. 35.

stepped into the mud were to wash his feet in mud.'[27] It was just as well for Heraclitus that he preached these doctrines in Ephesus rather than Athens, where no power on this earth could have prevented his being tried for impiety. Consider these remarks: 'The mysteries practised among men are unholy mysteries',[28] and 'Time is a child playing chess, moving the pieces about the board.'[29] Barely sixty years later, Socrates would be condemned to death for having said much less.

Historians have not always agreed about the basic views of Heraclitus. For some he is the philosopher of 'Fire', for whom this was the primordial element from which everything sprang and into which it will eventually return. Others have seen him as the philosopher of 'Becoming', because he held that everything was in an eternal state of flux. The most essential difference between these two interpretations is that the first assumes an eventual victor, fire, whereas the second assumes a drawn match, on the basis that neither side has anything to gain by the destruction of its opponent. To set the record straight, I frankly declare my own allegiance to the theory of 'Becoming'.

Reality, according to Heraclitus, is a ceaseless flow and transformation. There is nothing, animate or inanimate, that is not subject to constant change. Even material objects that seem at first sight to be static yield, on closer examination, signs of alteration. An iron bell is subject to rust, a cliff erodes, a tree grows, a man ages. *Panta rei*, all things are flowing. 'You cannot step twice into the same river.'[30] The symbol of this eternal flux is fire, Heraclitus' primary substance. 'All things are an exchange for fire, and fire for all things, even as wares for gold and gold for wares.'[31]

Now, although Ephesus is only forty kilometres from Miletus, and even if the definition of fire as the primary substance seems not far removed from the cosmological theories of Thales, Anaximander and Anaximenes, we must beware of falling into the trap of including Heraclitus among the philosophers of the Milesian school. In the field of speculative philosophy our cantankerous thinker did, in fact, despite

[27]R. P. 49 a.
[28]R. P. 48.
[29]R. P. 40 a.
[30]R. P. 33.
[31]R. P. 35.

his unamiable character, accomplish an enormous advance in respect of his predecessors.

The originality of Heraclitus' thinking lies in the concept of the world as a vast battlefield where all the forces are more or less equal. Struggle is not the exception but the norm, and men must accept it as a form of natural justice. 'War is common to all and strife is justice, and all things come into being and pass away through strife.'[32] 'War is the father of all things.'[33]

The philosopher railed at Homer because the poet had exclaimed (in the *Iliad*): 'Would that strife might perish from among gods and men!'[34] Did he not realize, storms Heraclitus, that he was praying for the destruction of the earth? What would be left if there were no strife? Utter desolation. 'Is it not sickness that makes health pleasant; evil, good; hunger, plenty; weariness, rest?'[35] One of the strangest and possibly most significant of Heraclitus' utterances was: 'The bow is called life, but its work is death.'[36] Explanation: in Greek both 'bow' and 'life' are expressed by the one word *bios*, not entirely coincidentally since the drawn bow, though apparently static, symbolizes life through the tension between the wood and the string, whereas the function of the bow is, of course, to inflict death. Woe to any warring element that achieves victory over its opposite: the result would be suicide for the victor. Were he alive today and living in America, Heraclitus would strongly advise the Democrats against trying to crush the Republicans since the total disappearance of the latter would imply the simultaneous collapse of the former.

For Heraclitus, the apparent chaos of the cosmic conflict concealed a rational order which he defined in a single word: *Logos*. And here we enter very deep water, because this word is capable of any number of interpretations. It can mean, quite simply, Language, but it can also mean Truth, Reason, Word, Reality or even God. My own belief is that Heraclitus used the word *Logos* to imply the natural law which governs the strife between the elements, without, however, implying any

[32]Fr. 62. in Bywater's numbering.
[33]R. P. 34.
[34]R. P. 34 d. Cf. *Iliad* xviii. 107.
[35]R. P. 48 b.
[36]R. P. 49 a.

metaphysical significance. For the Stoics, on the other hand, and for those who wanted to give a religious slant to the utterings of Heraclitus, the word *Logos* represented the will of the Creator. Stoic philosophy, and subsequently Christian thought, was never, unfortunately, able to free itself from the idea of a 'happy ending' as compensation for all the miseries of life on earth, and this involved a considerable distortion of the meaning. The principal argument in favour of a naturalistic interpretation is that no pre-Socratic philosopher was able to imagine anything non-material. Anaximander's *apeiron*, for example, was not immaterial like, say, a soul, but a substance, albeit a substance of a much, much more rarefied nature than air; and Pythagoras even thought of numbers as tiny objects extended in space.

The philosopher's own 'obscurity' is partly to blame for the problems of interpretation. Given the impenetrable nature of the fragments, anyone who has wanted to has been able to enlist Heraclitus' support for all his own pet theories, because, like statistics, they can be made to prove anything. I would advise students of philosophy to quote Heraclitus on every possible occasion. Never mind whether the question is about Hobbes, Spencer, Hegel, Bergson, Heidegger, Nietzsche or whomever, the 'Dark Philosopher' serves for them all, having said everything and the opposite of everything; it always makes a good impression and the risk is negligible.

Even Heraclitus had his fans, and these, as is generally the case, proved to be more fanatical than the master himself. Where Heraclitus said that it was impossible to bathe twice in the same river, his favourite disciple Cratylus maintained that one could not do so even once, and with regard to the futility of trying to communicate with one's fellow men, Cratylus' habit was to observe a total silence. When asked a question, his only reply was to waggle his little finger.

EXERCISE: The sun is as big as the foot of a man. *Discuss.*

IX
Tonino Capone

mong the many commonplaces that make conversation more banal than it need be is the particularly abominable one that exhorts us to 'look at life philosophically'. I do realize that being trapped in a lift for an hour is an experience that demands an acquaintance with philosophy if for no other reason than to while away the time; nevertheless, I still object to philosophy being relegated to a simple exercise in resignation. To have a philosophy means, among other things, to possess a sense of values on the basis of which we make our day to day decisions.

Take Tonino Capone as a case in point. We are in Naples, it's a July morning coming up to midday, the temperature has touched its seasonal zenith, my Fiat is parked in the sun. I climb into the sizzling car, turn the key in the ignition and then realize the battery's flat: I utter a loud oath and set off on foot towards the nearest supplier of electrical spares. Here I find the grille lowered and a notice on it which reads: HAVING EARNED AS MUCH AS HE NEEDS TONINO HAS GONE TO THE BEACH.

Tonino's decision is one which presupposes a philosophy worth analysing. We shall.

I first met Antonio Capone in 1948 at a theological college. He was a student there, I just went along to play football. At that time Tonino was an active lad, not a thinker; there was no hint that he would ever become a philosopher.

Having abandoned the ecclesiastical life even before embarking upon it, Tonino discovered two absorbing interests: football and engines. Cars, motorcycles, mopeds, motorboats – anything that possessed a combustion engine fascinated him. He left university and became a racing-car mechanic: he was always covered in grease and stank of castor oil. He married very young and found a job with Fiat in Naples as a test engineer, but marriage and job were both short lived and at the age of twenty-four he was again single and unemployed. In 1955 he took part in the Grand Prix of Posillipo driving a prototype of his own design. The race was won by Ascari and Tonino left the circuit at the first bend: had it not been for a dozen or so bales of straw and a small magnolia tree, he would have finished up in the sea after a precipitous flight of some two hundred metres. He broke both legs but no spectator was injured. Throughout the period when his legs were in plaster, the combined effects of immobility and his previous studies of Latin and Greek encouraged him to reread classical authors and take an interest in philosophy. Today Tonino is the only Italian intellectual I know capable of adjusting the contact-breakers in a distributor.

'Daily life,' said Tonino, 'is like a game of Monopoly. At the start every player receives twenty-four counters of liberty, one for each hour of the day. The object of the game is to use them to the best possible advantage.'

We were sitting in a pizzeria in the Vomero district of Naples. It was past one o'clock in the morning, all the customers had gone and the place was about to close. The proprietor, '*o mare-sciallo*, was counting the day's takings at the till while two waiters went from table to table removing the cloths and piling them on the floor ready to be taken to the laundry. In the corner, each with a cup of coffee in front of us, Tonino, Carmine (the elderly waiter) and myself were still sitting around a table.

'In order to live,' said Tonino, 'we need two things: a little money to make us economically independent, and a little affection to help us survive moments of loneliness unscathed. Neither of these comes gift-wrapped: they have to be bought, and the high price you have to pay is hours and hours of liberty. Southern Italians, for example, tend to go for a safe job and a regular wage packet. I'm not suggesting they want a job that's particularly demanding; quite the opposite in fact, but any employment, in terms of liberty, is one of the costliest things out. Eight hours a day means eight counters that must be paid out, even without overtime and an extra job on the side, maybe. And with regard to affection, here too a man will take the line of least resistance; he gets himself a wife and expects her to provide him with the measure of affection he needs. But this solution also has its price. At best, he's waving goodbye to another six hours of expendable liberty. As soon as a man gets home from work, his wife claims his attention. Let's do some adding up, now: eight hours for work, six for the wife, ten left over; and he's still got to sleep, wash, eat and travel to and from his place of work.'

'Donn'Antò,' said Carmine, who, not being an intimate friend, always addresses Tonino as *Donn'Antonio*, 'the only thing I don't understand is this business of the counters. Are you saying that in order to earn money a man must fork out . . .'

'Effectively yes,' interrupted Tonino. 'But we're talking about imaginary money and banknotes stand for hours of free time. If you sacrifice all the hours in the day to your work and your wife, you won't be left with even a moment to be on your own.'

'I see, Donn'Antò,' said Carmine, sounding unconvinced. 'But look, when I'm working I'm never bored, when I'm with my wife I am, let's say, a little bit bored, but it's when I'm alone that I really get bored and wonder if I wouldn't be better off at work.'

'That's because you've never learnt to be on your own. Do you know what a German philosopher called Nietzsche once said? "O solitude, my kingdom!"'

'They may like it in Germany,' objected Carmine, 'but solitude has never been very popular in Naples.'

'Solitude itself is neither good nor bad,' insisted Tonino. 'It's like an enlarging lens. If you're unhappy and alone you become very unhappy; if you're happy and alone you're very happy.'

'The trouble is that one is unhappy most of the time,' murmured Carmine.

'Anyway, I wasn't talking about solitude but about free time. And let's get one thing clear: everyone is at liberty to spend his free time in whatever way he likes. Some people like to stay at home alone, reading or thinking; others prefer to go out for a meal with friends; some even choose to spend their time in the car, driving about town. The important thing is that everyone should have some time, some little corner of the day, when he can do something different from making or spending money. In this day and age, unfortunately, consumerism is becoming increasingly dictatorial and now imposes its own rules of behaviour upon everybody, requiring people to do more than they really need to. If we could only eliminate superfluous expense, we could do away with the drudgery of overwork once and for all.'

'Donn'Antò!' Carmine exclaimed. 'That's hardly an argument that holds water for the likes of me! What superfluous expenses are you talking about? You're a bachelor, you've only got yourself to think about, but I'm a married man with three children. You get twenty thousand lire for putting a new bulb in a headlamp, but for me to earn six hundred thousand means a month's work and relying on generous tips.'

'Do you run a car?' asked Tonino rather sharply.

'If you can call it a car. I've got a beaten-up Fiat 127,' admitted Carmine, lowering his voice almost as if he felt guilty about it.

'But you don't consider that a superfluous expense. Yet your father never had a car and that didn't make his life any less happy than yours. Admit it: you bought the car because you saw other people had them, not because you really needed it. Isn't that so?'

'How can one possibly live in Naples without a car? The public transport's worse than useless!'

'Tell me, how would you define a rich man?'

'Someone who earns a lot of money.'

'How much?'

'Oh, I don't know . . . let's say three million lire a month.'

'Wealth, my dear Carmine, is not a particular sum of money in relation to which you can say that someone is rich because he earns more or poor because he earns less. Wealth is relative. If someone earns more than he spends, he's rich; and vice versa: if someone needs more than he earns, he's poor.'

'Come again,' said *'o maresciallo* who, having finished cashing up the till, had joined us at the table.

'I mean, wealth is only a state of mind: one can feel rich without having a lot of money. The important thing is to spend less than one earns and not to want what one hasn't got.'

'And that's the fly in the ointment, Donn'Antò: wanting things one hasn't got!' burst out Carmine. 'For instance, I desperately want a colour television, but they cost nearly a million. A million! How could I ever save up a million? Last Sunday I got eleven draws on the pools, but I ask you, ten minutes from the end Fiorentina goes and scores three-nil and wrecks everything!! So just tell me that I, Carmine Cascone, will never be able to buy a colour television, and I'll forget about it.'

'Of course,' said Tonino, 'no one can do without a colour television today.'

'They can, but I've had a real stroke of bad luck,' Carmine replied. 'And I'll tell you what happened. Right opposite where I live in Materdei there's a social club, the *Benedetto Croce*, where they've got a twenty-three-inch colour set. Now, because my wife used to be, as you might say, in charge of the domestic offices there, I used to be able to go and watch the football every Sunday afternoon. Then the club suddenly went broke and as well as not paying the rent, they sold the pool table they had on hire, so the makers sued them and the bailiffs arrived the other day and sealed the premises. But I've got into the habit now of seeing colour television and black-and-white just isn't the same any more. That's why I've simply got to buy a colour set.'

'If I were in your shoes, Carminiè, I'd sue the club,' suggested *'o maresciallo*, trying to keep a straight face. 'To all intents and purposes, they've behaved towards you like drug-pushers. First they gave it to you for nothing and now you have to pay for it.'

'Marescià, you're joking, but Carminiello would be absolutely in the right,' retorted Tonino. 'Seriously, because after what he told us just now, it's clear that the club, by its permissiveness, got him hooked on a higher life-style to the detriment of his relative wealth. Let me give you an example. Just suppose that you were to fire Carmine some day soon . . .'

'Not altogether unlikely,' interposed '*o maresciallo*, 'when he spends more time chatting with the customers than serving them pizzas.'

'. . . and just suppose that poor Carmine came to me to ask for a job . . .' continued Tonino, ignoring all interruptions.

'Donn'Antò, I'd better warn you that I know nothing about cars or electrics,' Carmine interjected.

'. . . and that I, for the sake of long acquaintance, told him that I needed a personal secretary and would take him on at a salary of a million and a half per month . . .'

'*Fosse 'a Madonna!*' sighed Carmine.

'. . . for the first year, but for the second and all subsequent years, for personal reasons the salary would have to be reduced to one million.'

'What?' protested Carmine. 'A million and a half the first year and only one million the next? What are you trying to do, Donn'-Antò, going down instead of up? I'm surprised at you. After one year a good employee has a right to a wage-rise.'

'But I'm a lunatic: I pay more the first year and less the year after,' insisted Tonino. 'And by so doing I ruin you. Because, you see, during the first year you would have got used to living on a million and a half, and for the rest of your life you would feel underpaid. But if you were clever, what would you do? During the first year you would take the extra half-million and give it to the beggar at the corner by the church. Then at the end of the year you wouldn't have to worry because you could carry on exactly as before; the only one to suffer would be the beggar on the corner who'd be wondering whatever happened to the kind gentleman who gave him half a million every month.'

'In fact,' Carmine admitted, 'the poor devil would have loosened his belt a bit. Who knows, he might even have found himself a girl-friend!'

'So, you see, the parable of the poor man receiving charity can help you to understand the secret of well-being,' Tonino concluded triumphantly. 'Wealth is only an attitude of mind: it's enough to want nothing in order to feel we're rolling in money. If you want to be happy, remember that happiness is the same thing as personal liberty. For myself, I have already reduced my life-style to a minimum. This means that I only need to work half the day and I can spend the rest of my time cultivating my friends and studying the world.'

Tonino Capone has never written a book. The only authenticated fragments are those in his business diary, where, between entries like 'Tuesday 18.30 Avv. Pittalà deadlocks' and 'Order Tudor batteries', every now and then one comes across a sentence such as: 'Much research goes into trying to lengthen life, when what we need to know is how to widen it.'

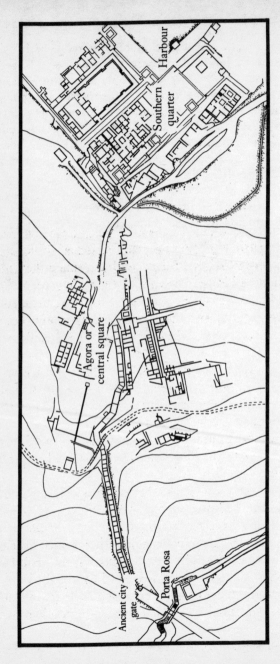

Fig. 4: Elea in ancient times

X
Elea

f only tourists, and especially Neapolitan tourists, could be persuaded against congesting the roads of Ischia with their cars and to venture instead slightly further south to explore the little known coastline between Punta Licosa and Capo Palinuro, sooner or later they would stumble across a little fishing village called Marina di Ascea where, apart from a sea of immemorial beauty, they would find, enveloped in an enchanted silence, the ancient walls of the city of Elea.

To the Phocaean colonists who first saw the place in that far-off year of 540 BC, it must have seemed the answer to all their prayers. It had a river, the Alento, wide and deep enough for a harbour, two islets, Pontia and Isacia,[1] guarding the estuary like sentinels, and a promontory jutting out into the sea and just waiting for an Acropolis to be built upon it. The Phocaeans knew at once that they had arrived at their journey's end.

At this point it might be useful to follow one of these odysseys from the beginning, because, among other things, it will help us to understand the reasons which drove our ancestors into such dangerous undertakings. Just imagine what it must have been like to cross the Mediterranean in a rowing boat in the sixth century BC! I have deliberately chosen the settlement of Elea by the Phocaeans as my example because these people were responsible more than any others for the dissemination of colonies throughout the known world. The

[1]Pliny, *Natural History* III 85.

Phocaeans have been credited with the exploration of the Adriatic Sea, the colonization of the Spanish coast and even, in the wake of Colaeus, a trip along the Atlantic coastline beyond the Pillars of Hercules.[2]

It all began on one black day in 545 BC or thereabouts, when a Persian general, Harpagus, bent upon occupying the Ionian coast in the name of Cyrus the Great, laid siege to the city of Phocaea (see fig. 2).

The history of man, prior to the invention of the aeroplane, consisted almost entirely of sieges. When a group of people decided to form a settlement, their first priority was to find a hill site that gave it a height advantage over invaders, then they built the walls. So great was the fear of ending one's days in slavery that the citizens of Ecbatana (now Hamadan) protected their city with no less than seven concentric rows of walls.[3] Phocaea had the added advantage of an escape route, the sea, especially handy for a race of excellent sailors whose 'fifty-oared galleys' were swift enough to outdistance almost any pursuer.

But let's return to the siege. Herodotus tells us[4] that after innumerable attempts to take the city had failed, Harpagus sent word to the Phocaeans that the conquest was merely a matter of prestige, so why not make a deal: the destruction of a single bastion would be enough for him to claim that Phocaea, too, had yielded to Cyrus. The Phocaeans took a day to consider this proposal and countered with one of their own, that the Persian troops should withdraw while they deliberated. Harpagus agreed and the entire population seized their chance and escaped by sea, bearing away with them all their wealth and even the statues of their gods.

A voyage undertaken on the spur of the moment and with the Persians in hot pursuit could obviously not be one of long duration, and the Phocaeans disembarked that very same night at nearby Chios, where, cash in hand, they offered to buy the Oenussae islands. Unfortunately for them, the inhabitants of Chios, afraid of possible

[2]Herodotus, *The Histories* IV 152.
[3]Herodotus, *op. cit.* I 98.
[4]Herodotus, *op. cit.* I 165.

competition for trade, turned them down, and the refugees found themselves obliged to take to their ships once more. Some of them, overcome by nostalgia, returned to their homes, others took their courage in both hands and headed west towards the distant island of Corsica, where the colony of Alalia (now Aleria) had been founded a few years previously by fellow Phocaeans.

Their arrival was distinctly unwelcome to the Carthaginians and Etruscans, who saw this continual influx of Ionians as a potential menace and decided to rid themselves of it once and for all. A large-scale naval battle ensued which was won by neither side – a Cadmean victory, as it used to be called.[5] The Phocaeans lost forty ships, many of the men were killed in the fighting, and those who managed to swim ashore were immediately stoned to death by the Corsicans, who even in those distant times were a people of few words. According to Herodotus, 'The result of this outrage was that when any living thing – sheep, ox or man – subsequently passed the place . . . its body became twisted and crippled by a paralytic stroke.'[6]

The survivors of the ill-fated expedition split into two groups: one founded Massalia (Marseilles),[7] the other went south to Rhegium (Reggio Calabria). The latter received a message from the Python advising them to make all haste and move further up the coast to the mouth of the river Alento. This colony was first called Hyele,[8] after the name of a spring there, then Elea and finally, by the ancient Romans, Velia, which is the name you should look for on the road maps.

The ground upon which the Acropolis was built is no longer a promontory because over the years alluvial deposits have added so much to the land around the estuary that the two islets, Pontia and

---

[5]The Greek equivalent to a 'Pyrrhic victory'. The allusion is to Cadmus, the mythological founder of Thebes, who, having slain the dragon guarding the fountain of Dirce, in Boeotia, sowed its teeth, from which armed men sprang up with intent to kill him. By the counsel of Athena, he threw a precious stone among them and they killed each other in the struggle to gain it. (*Brewer's Dictionary of Phrase and Fable*).

[6]Herodotus, *op. cit.* I 167.

[7]Strabo, *Geographica* IV 179.

[8]Strabo, *op. cit.* IV 252.

Isacia, have become joined to the mainland; they are still visible, however, as limestone outcrops in an otherwise purely alluvial zone. Approaching along the secondary road from Casal Velino, the traveller will see a signpost on his left bearing the legend 'per Velia', and a few hundred metres on, the walls of the lower city. One can see any number of German, French and even Japanese tourists, all naturally toting cameras; Italian tourists, however, are only notable by their absence. Were Elea in the Seychelles, perhaps it would be better known in those Italian social circles that matter; but you, my very dear citizens of Naples, you who are notorious for your cold-shouldering of the jet set, how can you stay away? Bring your family here one Sunday, and when you reach Porta Marina, remove your shoes and approach the Acropolis barefoot. As you enter the Porta Rosa you will be treading the same stones that were brushed by the sandals of Xenophanes two thousand five hundred years ago.

Down there in Elea today, all is peaceful, silent. Lie on the grass and consume the bread and *salsicce* and the *friarielli* so kindly prepared by your womenfolk; then sit quietly in the warm sun on the steps of the temple, contemplating the spot where, every morning, Parmenides taught Zeno that 'what is, is' and 'what is not, is not'; maybe the enchantment of your surroundings will help you to penetrate the philosophy of Being better than any scholarly treatise.

The remains of the walls show that Elea was never a great metropolis even in its heyday; and yet, in this small town of Campania, a school of philosophy came into being that was eventually to become a cornerstone in the history of western thought.

XI
Xenophanes

enophanes was a rhapsode and a singer of his own poems. His repertoire included the works of Homer and certain satires, called *silloi*, which he wrote to make fun of his colleagues. Whenever there was a social gathering, or symposium, Xenophanes was the first to be invited and nearly always, at the end of the banquet, someone would ask him to perform. 'Xenni,' they said, 'sing us the bit about Agamemnon stealing the slave girl from Achilles.' But eventually, having been asked to sing about the same episodes over and over again, he came to dislike Homer and from then on never had a good word for him. For the Greeks, however, Homer meant everything: no boy could consider his education complete until he knew his Homer inside out, and King Alcinous even suggested that the Gods had planned the whole tragic fall of Troy just so that Homer could 'make a song for future generations'.[1]

Xenophanes was a moralist, but – tempering vice with virtue – he also had a sense of humour. He criticized everything: besides Homer, he had it in for Hesiod, Thales, Pythagoras, Epimenides and everyone who was more famous than himself. He even, on one occasion, moaned about sportsmen: 'It is not just,' he said, 'that a boxer or an athlete who competes in the pentathlon and displays swiftness of foot should be honoured above the teacher of wisdom which, in my opinion, is of greater value than the physical strength of men or horses.'[2] And to

[1] *The Odyssey* VIII 578.
[2] Diels-Kranz fr. 2.

think that champions were not even sponsored in those days!

As to his qualities as a humorist, I have certain reservations; even after making allowances for the passing of twenty-five centuries, his witticisms are hardly earth-shattering. When someone once told him that he had seen eels living in hot water, he replied: 'Then I suppose when we want to cook them we should use cold water.'[3] Well, well. Still, who knows, maybe in another two thousand five hundred years scholars will be studying fragments of my own *Thus Spake Bellavista* in a similarly critical way.

Xenophanes, son of Dexius or Orthomenes, was also born on the Ionian coast, but at Colophon. While we are uncertain as to the name of his father, we fare no better in the matter of his date of birth: Diogenes (quoting Sotion) suggests that he was contemporary with Anaximander[4] (b. 610), while Clement of Alexandria[5] makes him contemporary with Hieron (tyrant of Gela in 470). For both to be right he would have had to live for more than one hundred years. And he may have done just that. All we know for certain is the account he himself gives us in an elegy: 'There are by this time threescore years and seven that have tossed my careworn soul up and down the land of Hellas; and there were then five-and-twenty years from my birth.'[6] We only have to do some simple addition: $67 + 25 = 92$, throw in a few extra years for good measure and there we are: one hundred. Notice that he speaks of his soul as already careworn at twenty-five. If this is a reference to his exile, then, bearing in mind that the Median invasion took place in 540, he must have been born in 565 or thereabouts.

Apparently self taught, Xenophanes was at odds with the world as soon as he reached the age of reason. In the first half of the sixth century Colophon was governed by an oligarchy, reputedly consisting of a troop of one thousand horsemen, and was under the jurisdiction of Lydia. There was nothing unusual about this, yet the tenuous Lydian domination displeased the young Xenophanes, who considered the soldiers of Croesus to be playboys and blamed them for the increasing moral laxity of his fellow citizens. He was forced to rethink his opinions

---

[3]Plutarch, *Apophthegmata* 46; 1084 F.
[4]Diogenes Laertius, *op. cit.* IX 18.
[5]Clement of Alexandria, *Stromata* I 64.
[6]Diels-Kranz, fr. 8.

of the Lydians by Harpagus, the military leader of the Medes, a soldier of the old sort and terror of the Ionian coast. When this new army of occupation arrived, the philosopher saw immediately that reciting satires was not going to be the in thing, and made himself scarce forthwith.

He then went through a very rough patch: he fell into the hands of pirates, who sold him into slavery, and was freed by the Pythagoreans Parmeniscus and Orestades,[7] he buried his sons with his own hands,[8] and he roamed ceaselessly, turning up in Zankle (Messina), Catana,[9] Malta, Syracuse,[10] Agrigento and Lipari[11] where, we are told, he was fascinated by a volcanic eruption (but which volcano? He may have confused Stromboli with Lipari). So he led a wandering life until he arrived in Elea, and here, according to some, he settled for a time and founded a school.

At the time of his death he was old and poor, so poor that he once confessed he 'could no longer afford even to keep two slaves'.[12]

Apart from the *silloi* and elegies, he wrote a poem in hexameters entitled *De Natura* and two others on historical subjects: *The Founding of Colophon* and *The Settlement of a Colony at Elea in Italy*.

Some histories of philosophy mention Xenophanes as the first, chronologically speaking, of the Eleatics. Now, there is little doubt that he lived in Elea, and we know for a fact that he was older than Parmenides, but even so, to declare him the founder of the Eleatic school of philosophy is maybe rather far-fetched. Perhaps the 'comic poet of Colophon'[13] should not be described as a philosopher at all but as a theologian born by some oversight seven centuries before his time. All credit is due to him, however, for having been the first to coin the slogan 'One God is All', thus – to some extent – foreshadowing Parmenides.

[7]Diogenes Laertius, *op. cit.* IX 20.
[8]Diogenes Laertius, *loc. cit.*
[9]Diogenes Laertius, *op. cit.* IX 18.
[10]Hippolytus, *op. cit.* I 14.
[11]Aristotle, *De divinatione* 38 833a 15.
[12]Plutarch, *Of Kings and Commanders*, 175 C.
[13]P. Tannery, *op. cit.*, p. 131.

Central to Xenophanes' thought is the idea that God should not be confused with the bunch of eccentrics that we find in the poems of Homer and Hesiod.[14] 'They have ascribed to the gods all things that are a shame and a disgrace among mortals, stealings and adulteries and deceivings of one another.'[15] God is a superior being, All and One. But beware: the expression 'one God' has none of the connotations that we, living in a Christian society long used to the concept of monotheism, might imagine. We are dealing here with a pantheistic theory of the same kind, for instance, as Thales', according to which everything is a god and the sum of everything is a Whole possessing the attributes of divinity. By contrast, ignorant mortals imagine the gods to be a race of supermen made in their own image and likeness: 'The Ethiopians make their gods black and snub nosed; the Thracians say theirs have blue eyes and red hair',[16] and 'If oxen and horses or lions had hands, and could paint with their hands, and produce works of art as men do, horses would paint the forms of the gods like horses, and women like oxen, and make their bodies in the image of their several kinds.'[17]

Firstly, says Xenophanes, when we speak of God we cannot say that he was born, because the perfect cannot be born of the imperfect. God is therefore unbegotten and eternal. And there cannot be a multitude of gods, because in that case some would be superior and some inferior, and the concept of an inferior god is not tenable. Nor could they be equal, because that would mean that none was better than the others, which would contradict the most essential prerogative of divinity, which is to be supreme. He concludes that God is One, Omnipotent and Spherical, and is therefore neither infinite nor finite.

Aristotle disagrees with Xenophanes about the spherical nature of God: 'To state that God is spherical is to impose limits upon him.'[18] A reconciliation of these conflicting views would eventually arrive at Einstein's theory of four-dimensional curved space that was both finite and infinite. But I am afraid of straying too far away from the

---

[14]Thus Xenophanes. We, on the other hand, are quite happy with Homer's anthropomorphic Gods.
[15]Diels-Kranz, fr. 11.
[16]Diels-Kranz, fr. 16.
[17]Diels-Kranz, fr. 15.
[18]Pseudo-Aristotle, *On Melissus, Gorgias and Xenophanes* 3, 977a.

down-to-earth treatment promised at the beginning, so I shall drop the subject and leave the above remarks stimulating the imagination of the reader.

While Xenophanes foreshadowed Parmenides by his suggesting the One-ness of God, his ideas on the physical world were closer to those of the Milesian school. 'All things,' he said, 'come from the earth, and in earth all things end.'[19] In its present state the world consists of earth and water and a mixture of the two, which is mud. As evidence of the intrusion of one element into the zone of another, the philosopher cited the fossil forms of fish, plants and shells found in the quarries of Syracuse.[20] One of his most extraordinary statements is that the earth beneath our feet is infinite,[21] not floating upon the water as suggested by Thales, nor suspended in the void as Anaximander chose to think.

The Xenophanes that has the greatest appeal for me is Xenophanes the poet. Let us read one of his elegies together and imagine ourselves guests at a banquet taking place in the fifth century BC.

'. . . Now is the floor clean, and the hands and cups of all; one sets twisted garlands on our heads, another hands us fragrant ointment on a salver. The mixing bowl stands ready, full of gladness, and there is more wine at hand that promises never to run dry, soft and smelling of flowers in the jars. In the midst the frankincense sends up its sacred perfume, and there is cold water, sweet and clean. Loaves are set before us and a lordly table laden with cheese and rich honey. The altar in the midst is clustered round with flowers; song and revel fill the halls. But first it is meet that men should hymn the God with joy, with sacred tales and pure words; then after libation and prayer made that we may have strength to do right, no sin is it to drink as much as a man can take and get home without an attendant, so he be not stricken in years . . .'[22]

[19]Diels-Kranz, fr. 27.
[20]Hippolytus, *Confutation of all Heresies* I 14.
[21]Diels-Kranz, fr. 28.
[22]Diels-Kranz, fr. 1.

XII
Parmenides

Parmenides, son of Pyres, was born in Elea between 520 and 510 BC. Diogenes Laertius tells us that he was a pupil of Xenophanes, Anaximander and Ameinias the Pythagorean.[1] There is little doubt about his having been a pupil of Xenophanes: the village in which they both lived boasted less than a thousand inhabitants, there were few distractions and they could hardly have helped knowing each other. The presence of Anaximander in the list of teachers, however, seems highly suspect: two thousand miles of sea and, above all, a difference of one hundred years between them should have made any contact wellnigh impossible. With regard to Ameinias, I fear that relations between the Pythagorean and the Eleatic may not have been entirely those of master and pupil. I have read Sotion's account[2] very carefully and noted that while the historian speaks of Parmenides as being 'a pupil of' Xenophanes, he uses the more ambiguous 'associated with' when it comes to Ameinias, and this, in some translations, even appears as 'intimate with'. Plato himself, in the *Parmenides*, confirms the homosexuality of the philosopher by introducing Zeno as his 'particular favourite'.[3] There is nothing especially remarkable about this: homosexuality was very common at the time and nearly every philosopher had his boy-friend. But these thinkers were also wont, unlike those of our own times, to frequent beautiful hetaeras.

[1] Diogenes Laertius, *op. cit.* IX 21.
[2] Diogenes Laertius, *op. cit. ibid.*
[3] Plato, *Parmenides* 127 A.

Parmenides was born into an illustrious and wealthy family and had a reputation for generosity. Ameinias was poor; when he died, Parmenides built a shrine to him and paid for it out of his own pocket.[4]

According to Plutarch his gifts as a legislator were so great that all his fellow citizens took an oath when they came of age to abide by the laws of Parmenides.[5]

He taught Zeno and Empedocles, and having said that I have exhausted all the facts I know about his life apart from the voyage to Athens in 450. This, it would appear, was some kind of diplomatic mission undertaken by the Eleatics with the object of persuading Pericles to sign a treaty of alliance between the two cities. In the event, Parmenides and Zeno spent less time with the politicians than with their Athenian colleagues. To all intents and purposes, this was a summit meeting of philosophers, with the Eleatics on one side determined to show that when it came to profundity of thought the province was at least the equal of the metropolis, and on the other side Socrates who, though only twenty-five at the time, was already an inexorable dialectician. The resulting discussion was the most complex and the dullest in the annals of philosophy. Plato gives an exhaustive account of it in the *Parmenides*, and despite his literary ability, I doubt if anyone has ever read this dialogue from beginning to end, not even the editor of my school book. When I say 'anyone' I am referring, of course, to normal people.

Having warned you, I'll give you a taste of the philosophers' conversation at this historic encounter by quoting the opening of Socrates' argument.[6] 'Do you mean to say, Zeno, that if reality is a "many", many things must be at once like and unlike – which is absolutely impossible, because the unlike can never be like, nor the like unlike? ... Since unlike cannot be like, nor like unlike, it must also be impossible that reality should be "many" because if it were ...' and so on for another fifty pages.

One's first impression is of a tongue-twister on the lines of 'Round the rugged rocks the ragged rascals ran', but obviously the more

---

[4]Diogenes Laertius, *op. cit. ibid.*
[5]Plutarch, *Adversus Colote* 1226 A.
[6]Plato, *Parmenides* 128 B. (Quoted in the translation by John Warrington, London 1961).

attentively one reads the passage, the more one begins to glimpse light at the end of the tunnel. The average man will usually get to page seven, where Parmenides says, 'Look now, suppose you split up Magnitude itself and say that every large thing is large by virtue of a part of Magnitude, which is less than Magnitude itself; won't your statement appear rather silly?' Socrates replies, 'Indeed!' and the average man also says 'indeed' and promptly dismisses Parmenides completely.

Now, I'm no long-distance runner when it comes to abstract ratiocination, and maybe I tend to give up rather easily; at the same time, however, I cannot help being amazed by the seriousness with which these philosophers of Magna Graecia approached abstract problems. Think about it. Two men, born and bred in a small town in the district of Cilento in the fifth century BC, arrive at a great city like Athens and here, instead of painting the town red, settle down to subtle philosophical disquisitions about similarity and dissimilarity; yet today, on the eve of the twenty-first century and in spite of the influence of television, in those selfsame townships in the south of Italy you can hardly sell a newspaper!

Parmenides set out his ideas in a poem entitled – as usual – *De Natura*.[7] The opening of the poem is very striking: the philosopher imagines himself riding in a chariot drawn by fiery mares (the passions of the soul) towards an abode 'far from the beaten track of men'.

> The axle glowed in the socket and gave forth a sound as of a pipe (being urged round by the whirling wheels at each end) as the daughters of the Sun left the abode of Night and hastened on towards the Light. There stands the Gate which divides the ways of Night and Day.

Here, Parmenides finds Avenging Justice guarding the Gate and refusing to relinquish the keys. But the Daughters of the Sun (the senses) persuade her 'with gentle words' to allow the poet to pass through and then conduct him into the presence of the Goddess. Severe yet benevolent, the Goddess greets him kindly and addresses him thus:

[7]Sextus Empiricus, *Adversus Mathematicos* VII 111.

It is meet that thou shouldst travel both roads: the unshaken heart of well-rounded truth (science), and the opinions of mortals (appearances) in which there is no true belief at all.

This was how Parmenides came to know the Truth and decide to reveal it to posterity. Now we must try to understand it.

To talk about 'becoming' in Parmenides' presence was like swearing in church. One risked a kick in the pants. His *idée fixe* was that the Truth (or the One, or God, or the Logos, or Being)[8] was 'one, complete, immovable and uncreated'.[9]

One, because only one reality can exist.

Complete, because there is no empty space and therefore nothing to divide the One into parts.

Immovable, because in order to move the One would have to occupy a space previously empty.

Uncreated, because something that *is* cannot arise from something which *is not*, and that which is not, by definition, does not exist.

The Goddess indicated that there were two roads leading to such a conclusion: the Way of Truth and the Way of Opinion. The first is identified with the One, and is the only reality that exists. The second is identified with the Many, and is only appearance.

Parmenides is an intellectual snob like most of his pre-Socratic colleagues, and like them he has a very low opinion of ordinary men: 'Two-faced mortals,' he called them, 'in whose breasts thought wanders deaf, blind, stupid and incapable of distinguishing what is from what is not, truth from opinion.'[10]

Thought, according to Parmenides, implies Being,[11] while not-being is unthinkable. To put it more clearly, if you can think of a thing, the thought itself proves that the thing exists, while not-being not only does not exist but cannot even be thought about. This is where I begin to have problems: if I think about Sophia Loren, obviously there must be a woman called Sophia Loren otherwise I

[8]Tick your choice of definition.
[9]Pseudo-Plutarch, *op. cit.* 5.
[10]Diels-Kranz fr. 6.
[11]Diels-Kranz fr. 5.

could not have thought about her. On the other hand, I could as well think about someone who no longer exists, like Totò for example, in which case the existence of the person should not be implied as of necessity. At most one could say: 'A man exists who is thinking about a comedian called Totò who is, unhappily, no longer with us.' But Parmenides would smile at my objection and tell me that I have confused 'being' and 'existing': Totò's being dead is a matter of appearance only and in reality Totò still 'is'. More determined than ever, I conjure up an image of something which not only 'is not' at present, but has never even 'existed'! I think, let's say, of an extra-terrestrial being uglier than E.T., with feet like a chicken's, a nose like an elephant's trunk, and ears like the Right Honourable Signor Andreotti's. But Parmenides is unimpressed. He says that if I can imagine this monster, then it 'exists'; and seeing that I am so fond of the verb 'to exist', I cannot deny that chickens, elephants' trunks and the Right Honourable Signor Andreotti all do in fact exist.

The strange thing about Parmenides is that every time he comes out with his 'What is, is, what is not, is not', my immediate reaction is scepticism; but then I remember that I'm dealing with one of the greatest of the Greek philosophers and bite my tongue. The same sort of thing happens when I look at a painting by Paul Klee: in the first instance my common sense tells me it's a meaningless daub, then the celebrity of the master and the solemnity of my surroundings end up by convincing me otherwise.

In painting, music and art in general, a work does not have to have an explicit meaning. Sometimes it is entirely self-contained, an aesthetic experience not intended to do anything apart from stir the emotions. Sadly, the majority of people are teleologists, which means that for them every single human action has to have a precise purpose, so the purpose and the meaning of a work of art are seen as identical. Having said that, I should not want to fall into the same error *vis-à-vis* Parmenides as the teleologists *vis-à-vis* abstract painting. Could it be, I ask myself, that this 'what is, is, what is not, is not' is only a poetic expedient to stimulate my ontological fantasies?

Ontology, the science or study of Being, is, in my opinion, the most difficult cliff to scale in the study of Greek philosophy. In some systems of Oriental thought, too, such as Taoism and Zen, I have found much the same difficulty, which leads me to think that both Taoism and Zen have something in common with the philosophy of Being. It is certainly not easy to find a practical application for ontology. Suppose someone were to ask me out of the blue: 'Professor, I have decided that from next Monday I shall live ontologically. Please give me some idea about how I should behave. Should I, for instance, continue to work at the office or not?' What could I say? Maybe I would suggest something on these lines: 'Behave normally but try to avoid all excess, negative and positive, in everyday life. If you get a parking ticket, or if Juventus wins against Napoli, control your emotional reaction by thinking of the essence of life.' In other words, I wouldn't have a clue.

Perhaps the first thing we should do as we try to understand Parmenides is to avoid writing 'what is, is . . .' with omission dots, as if we were really on the point of knowing how to define the damned thing and, instead, get into the habit of using the phrase as a simple statement: 'What is, is' full stop. But then, given our natural curiosity and hence reluctance to resign ourselves to the statement: 'What is, is, and more we must not ask', we could perhaps allow ourselves to enquire if there were not, maybe, some definition of Being, however inadequate, for us common mortals. We might try a definition of not-being and hope that this will enable us to deduce the more complex concept by antithesis.

Working on these lines, we could think of Not-being as a collective definition of the objects presented to our senses in the form of colour, taste, sound and so on, and of Being as the essence of the things themselves, the part that lurks 'underneath' the changeable appearance.

In his wonderful fable *Le petit Prince*, the French poet Antoine de Saint-Exupéry tells us that, as a boy, he lived in a house where there was supposed to be some buried treasure. The treasure was never found, but the very possibility lent a special quality of beauty to the place. 'We generally look only at the shell of things,' said Saint-Exupéry, 'and do not realize that the truly important part lies concealed.'

To those who heaped praises upon his head for having created such brilliant sculptures, Michelangelo had a habit of replying that all he had done was to remove the excess marble in the block. Applying this to our argument, appearances become the 'excess', and the ideal statue, imprisoned within the marble and unique in its perfection, is the Being that our imaginations are trying to grasp.

As you can see, our feet are now planted fairly and squarely on the road leading towards the region of the Platonic forms. But beware! This is a steep and slippery slope that might well land us in the ditch!

XIII
Zeno

eno was Parmenides' 'sidekick'. During the famous conference of philosophers in the house of Pythodorus in Athens, he was the one to get the ball rolling, to 'warm up the house' in theatrical parlance, and it was he who pinpointed the moment when the audience's attention had reached its *akmè* and then made a great show of having to implore the master to speak. 'I would not ask it of you,' he said, 'if there were more of us here, because the subject is not for discussion before a large company, particularly for a man of your years; but as it is, Parmenides, I join Socrates in his request to you to speak, and look forward myself to hearing you again after all this time.'[1] To which Parmenides, despite having come to the gathering for no other purpose than to air his ideas, agreed with great reluctance, saying: 'I feel rather like the horse in Ibycus' poem, trembling with fear at the start of the race because he knew what was coming, or like the poet himself, who compares himself to the horse because he feels he is too old to make love. In the same way, I dread the necessity of a voyage at my time of life through so formidable a sea of words. However, I must do my best ...' If *he* was afraid, how should *we*, not being philosophers, feel when forced to wade through page after page of abstract reasoning only to discover at the end that 'One is One and cannot be Many, whether the One is or is not'?[2]

[1]Plato, *Parmenides* 136.
[2]Plato, *Parmenides* 166.

Zeno, the son of Teleutagoras, was born in Elea around 490 BC.[3] Had he been born anywhere else, he would probably have become a good fisherman or at best a schoolmaster, but growing up as he did a stone's throw from the house of Parmenides, his intelligence and vivacity, even as a small boy, did not go unremarked. In those days the leaders of the politico-philosophical clans, such as Pythagoras for example, were always on the look-out for new talent to recruit, so it was natural for Parmenides, having realized the boy's potential, to enquire about adopting him. Zeno's parents, for their part, happily agreed to the proposal since Parmenides was considered a pillar of the local community. The rumour that the choice had as much to do with the physical attractions of the boy as with his intellectual gifts is one we cannot ignore, though in the absence of contemporary gossip columnists all we have to go on is the reference in Plato[4] already noted and a phrase in Diogenes Laertius describing Zeno as the 'pupil and bosom friend' of Parmenides.

The youth studied physics, mathematics and astronomy and within a short time acquired an exceptional culture. He was also a gifted polemicist, so good that Aristotle credited him with being the inventor of dialectic.[5] Among his numerous pupils were Melissus, Empedocles, Leucippus, Pythodorus, Cephalus, Callinus and even Pericles himself. According to Plato,[6] his private lessons were especially valuable, but not cheap: a whole course cost one hundred *minas*, the price a man of the time could have paid for a small plot of land.

Not all the authorities agree about Zeno's physical attractions or even about his general appearance. Was he, for instance, tall or short? Plato describes him as 'tall and graceful',[7] while an Arab historian, one Al-Mubassir, says that, although handsome, 'he was short and snub-nosed'.[8] Elsewhere we read that 'his eyes were magnificent, large, black and almond-shaped' but 'his head was large in proportion

---

[3] Diogenes Laertius, *op. cit.* IX 25.
[4] Plato, *Parmenides* 127.
[5] Aristotle, fr. 65 Rose.
[6] Plato, *Alcibiades* I 119 A.
[7] Plato, *Parmenides* 127.
[8] Cf. F. Rosenthal, *Arabische Nachrichten über Zenon den Eleaten, in* 'Orientalia' 6, 1937, pp. 21–67.

to his body and he had a birthmark on his cheek'. The historians cannot even find common ground in the matter of his deportment. Some tell us that he 'moved very slowly, taking care to carry his head very high', others maintain that 'when he set off, it was difficult to catch up with him because he walked so fast. He was in the habit of carrying a stick with a forked handle ornamented with ivory and emeralds.'[9]

Whether Zeno was handsome or not is, of course, neither here nor there, yet I must admit to being surprised at these great philosophers who could, at one and the same time, preach indifference to appearances and cosset their public image down to the last detail. And while we are on the subject, we should bear in mind that the Greek art of oratory, too, was more concerned with form than content. Fashion dictated the ponderous, sacerdotal walk, the solemn gesture, the sententious style. A visit to the Greek statues in the Vatican Museum shows one immediately how important it must have been at that time to create an impression that inspired respect.

For Zeno in particular the impression he made must have been a source of endless preoccupation. Like all politicians, he knew perfectly well that a gesture or a well-timed pause can be more eloquent at times than a long speech, and that people can be swayed by histrionics better than with argument – in spite of the Eleatic doctrine that dismissed appearance as a mere simulacrum.

Zeno's main hobby, politics, raised him to a position of high esteem in the community but was also the cause of his tragic end. It would seem – though this is by no means certain – that towards the end of the fifth century Elea had come under the dictatorship of a certain Nearchus, variously described as leader of the democratic party[10] or Tyrant of Syracuse.[11] Whatever he was, Zeno organized a plot against him. He financed an armed expedition of aristocrats which left the island of Lipari intending to disembark at night on the Italian coast. Unfortunately, things went wrong, probably due to the work of an informer. Before the revolutionaries had set foot upon the beach at

---

[9]M. Untersteiner, *Zenone. Testimonianze e frammenti,* Florence 1963.
[10]Philostratus, *Life of Apollonius of Tyana.*
[11]F. Rosenthal, *art. cit.*

Elea, they were set upon by Nearchus' men, most of them were killed and the philosopher was dragged in chains before the tyrant.

Tertullian tells us that a few years before the disaster, Zeno had been asked by another tyrant, Dionysius, what he considered the chief benefit to be derived from a study of philosophy, and had replied: 'Indifference to death'.[12] Now, on the very last day of his life, the old man had occasion to demonstrate the truth of his statement. Nearchus did everything in his power to wrest from him the names of the conspirators who had remained in Elea, and Zeno coolly named, one by one, all the tyrant's closest friends.[13] Only when the torture became unbearable did he promise to reveal the whole truth, and that only to Nearchus in private, and as the tyrant, anxious not to miss a single name, put his ear close to the philosopher's mouth, Zeno sank his teeth into it and held on until the torturers ran him through with their swords.[14] And he was not yet through: still not dead, he was tortured again, and this time he bit off his own tongue and spat it in the tyrant's face.[15] Nearchus got the message at last: there was nothing he could do to break a spirit such as this. So he ordered Zeno to be cast into a mortar and beaten to a pulp.[16]

Before he breathed his last, the philosopher is reported to have declared: 'Virtue is not sufficient in this life; one also needs the help of fortune.' As a maxim, this has never seemed an outstandingly original pronouncement, but since it was made with half a tongue from the depths of a mortar, it undoubtedly deserves to be recorded for posterity.[17]

Parmenides was always having his leg pulled,[18] and for a faithful disciple like Zeno, who from the little we know about him seems to have been particularly argumentative and touchy, this must have been a trial. The jokes made fun of the central principle of Eleaticism ('What is, is, what is not, is not') because of its basic logical

---

[12]Tertullian, *Apologeticus* 50.
[13]Diogenes Laertius, *op. cit.* IX 27.
[14]Diodorus Siculus, *op. cit.* X 18, 2.
[15]Clement of Alexandria, *op. cit.* IV 57.
[16]Diogenes Laertius, *op. cit.* IX 27.
[17]M. Untersteiner, *op. cit.*, p. 19.
[18]Plato, *Parmenides* 128.

inconsistency. How on earth, said the critics, can one possibly conceive what *is* if one has no idea of what *is not*? How can one hope to perceive the One without knowing the Many, or speak of Light if one has never experienced Dark? Since what *is* assumes, as a logical precondition, knowledge of what *is not*, let's finish Parmenides' sentence for him: 'What is, is, what is not, is not, even though its existence must be presumed.'

To combat such criticism, Zeno adopted a method which argued from the premises admitted by the other side and led, via logical exposition, to an absurd conclusion. At no point – and this was very important to him – did he fail to respect the principle of non-contradiction. Although we cannot consider Zeno as one of the major stars in the philosophical firmament, since his main role was that of apologist for Parmenides, the place he occupies in the history of philosophy as a dialectician is of primary importance, since he anticipated the methods of the Sophists and of Socrates himself. The main targets attacked by the Eleatics were plurality and motion. You, said Zeno to his critics, may laugh at the idea of the 'One', but I shall now show you the absurdities inherent in the idea of the 'Many'. And he stated his paradoxes.

First paradox:[19] Let us suppose that a man decides to drive from Naples to Rome along the Autostrada del Sole. Now, the philosopher will argue, our driver can never reach his destination because before reaching the Roma Sud exit he must cross the half-way point somewhere around Pontecorvo, and before reaching Pontecorvo he must cross another middle line, the Capua exit which marks the half-way point of the first half of the Autostrada, and before reaching Capua he must reach yet another half-way point and so on *ad infinitum*. In other words, any line can be divided into two halves, and each of these halves can be further subdivided into shorter and shorter sections, and no section will ever be small enough not to be subdivided. Thus, our driver travelling to Rome will have to traverse an infinite number of half-way points and in order to do this he will need an infinite amount of time, so he can never arrive at his journey's end.

[19]Aristotle, *Physics* VI 9, 239b 9.

Second paradox:[20] Achilles, as we all know, was a swift runner, yet according to Zeno he could never have caught up with the slowest tortoise. Imagine Achilles sitting at point A and the stationary tortoise looking at him from point B. Suddenly the Greek hero decides to catch the tortoise so he jumps up and swoops like a falcon towards point B. The tortoise, realizing that Achilles means him no good, decides to make himself scarce, and in the time that it takes Achilles to get from A to B, manages to crawl a few centimetres to point C. Achilles, puzzled, wonders why he has not been able to catch him, and convinced of his own superiority, sets off again for point C. But the tortoise has moved again, and in spite of his slowness, has got to point D. This could go on for ever: Achilles will never catch up with the tortoise unless it drops dead (but tortoises are known for their longevity) or decides to wait for him somewhere along the way.

Third paradox:[21] An archer shoots an arrow towards the target, we all see it fly through the air except Zeno, who maintains the contrary. At any one moment, he argues, the arrow is at rest, and no amount of adding up moments of rest will produce movement.

If he were living today, Zeno would tell us to photograph the arrow in flight and then tell him if it were at rest or not. Theoretically, we may concede the logic of the argument, but even so I would most earnestly recommend my readers not to stand in the path of flying arrows.

Fourth paradox:[22] Three boys, Antonio, Gennaro and Pasquale, go to the athletics stadium. The first two go out on the track and start running, one clockwise, the other anticlockwise, while the third, not feeling like taking any exercise, finds a seat in the middle of the stand. At the end of a lap, Antonio and Gennaro meet and pass each other right in front of Pasquale. As they do so, Antonio's speed seems twice as great to Gennaro, who is running in the opposite direction as it does to Pasquale, who is stationary. Zeno, who believes in the principle of non-contradiction, therefore says: 'Because movement appears different to different observers, it does not exist!'

[20]Aristotle, *Physics* VI 9, 239b 14.
[21]Aristotle, *Physics* VI 9, 239b 30.
[22]Aristotle, *Physics* VI 9, 239b 33.

Of the four paradoxes, the last is the simplest to explain, so simple, I venture to suggest, that it hardly qualifies as a paradox. We have learnt from the theory of relativity that it makes no sense to describe an object as moving unless we specify that it is moving relative to something else. So it comes as no surprise to us that the speed of Antonio should be 15 m.p.h. relative to Pasquale (who is stationary) and 30 m.p.h. relative to Gennaro (who is running in the opposite direction). According to Einstein, both hypotheses are correct. But a fifth-century pedant like Zeno, who had never travelled on a train and seen the trees racing towards him, was understandably impressed by a phenomenon which we, who know all about relativity, take for granted.

The remaining three paradoxes, however, all spring from a common source: the problem of the infinite divisibility of finite time and space. Most textbooks again drag in relativity saying that Zeno's brain-teasers can only be resolved within a four-dimensional space–time context. However, I should like to avoid snatching my reader from the frying pan of Zeno only to cast him into the fire of Einstein, so I shall do my best to explain the absurdities of Zeno's paradoxes by a kind of 'dog-mathematics'.

Zero and Infinity are numbers like all the others, maybe not in everyday use with people such as you or me, yet common enough in equations and mathematical formulae. These strange numbers do, however, have characteristics peculiar to themselves: zero, multiplied by whatever number, is always zero, and the same goes for infinity, too. What, you might ask, happens if we multiply Zero by Infinity? The answer is that nothing happens. Any conjunction of these mathematically qualified expressions will produce a drawn match, an undefined quantity.

Take the first paradox. If I subdivide a stretch of road (i.e. a finite length) an infinite number of times, at the 'end' (in inverted commas) I shall have an infinite number of sections of road each of zero length. Having said that, I cannot affirm, as Zeno does, that the sum of these segments is necessarily infinite, since the segments in question, though infinite in number, are also zero in length. Therefore, to say that 'the sum of an infinite number of zeros is infinite' is a nonsense: it is to declare Infinity the winner of our match and Zero the loser.

In the second paradox, too, the tortoise has to travel over sections of ground that become progressively smaller and smaller, so the sections he covers will, practically speaking, eventually be of zero length – at which point Achilles will catch him and give him the boot up the backside he deserves.

And finally, with regard to the paradox of the arrow in flight, I have nothing to add except to point out that here we are dealing not only with space but with time, which Zeno amused himself by subdividing into an infinite number of instants each equal to zero. Same reasoning, same conclusion.

I trust I have made myself clear. If not, no matter, because one can manage excellently even without the paradoxes of Zeno.

Antisthenes the Cynic, for instance, couldn't stand the Eleatics and their arguments against motion. One day, so the story goes,[23] having failed to rebut Zeno's paradox about the arrow, he started pacing up and down the room until the philosopher snapped:

'Keep still, for heaven's sake!'

'So,' murmured Antisthenes, 'you admit that I am moving?'

---

[23]Proclus, *In Parmenidem* I p. 694 23.

XIV
Melissus

elissus is the only man in history to have combined the roles of naval commander and philosopher. Members of the armed forces, and naval men in particular, are generally better at barking orders than engaging in dialectic; still, in spite of that, Melissus managed to secure himself a niche in the history of philosophy as the fourth and last of the Eleatic thinkers. How he managed to reconcile the immobility of the Parmenidean universe with the bursts of military activity required of him as a strategos will always be a mystery; however, there is something very appealing in the picture of the commander on the bridge of his flagship, crouched over a hatchway and scribbling away at his book *On Nature and Reality* on a calm day off the Ionian coast.

We know little or nothing of the life of Melissus. Plutarch[1] tells us that he was in command of the Samian fleet when it scored a victory over the Athenians, and this may well be the reason why our information about him is so sketchy. Athens, in the second half of the fifth century, was the keystone of the Greek world, and to attack her was to risk effacement from the pages of history, certainly as far as the leading men of culture at the court of Pericles were concerned. A couple of generations later, their work of censorship was completed by Aristotle, and then no one got away with it: the encyclopaedic philosopher of Stagirus, like the perfect computer that he was, catalogued, evaluated and laid down for the next two thousand years who

---

[1]Plutarch, *Life of Pericles* XXVI.

was worthy of surviving in the annals of history and who should be consigned to oblivion.

He had no mercy on Zeno and Melissus and dismissed them both as charlatans. He detested the former for his paradoxes and the second for having conferred upon matter the attribute of infinity which, to his way of thinking, should have been reserved for the category of the ideal. Whatever the judgements handed down by Plato and Aristotle, no evaluation of the pre-Socratic philosophers has been able to ignore them. So few of the original texts have survived that experts in the field have been forced to rely upon these two great white chiefs and to accept all they said on the subject as gospel, but we all know what happens in such cases: historians can be solid as rock when dealing with remote events, but God help us all and save us from the judgements of our own colleagues.

Melissus, son of Ithaegenes,[2] was born on the island of Samos between 490 and 480 BC. We know nothing about the first forty years of his life, but as he was an admiral we are entitled to assume that he made a number of sea voyages. He probably visited Miletus and Elea, for these were the places where, respectively, Anaximander and Parmenides, the philosophers who had the greatest influence upon him, had lived and worked. But the theory that he met the Eleatics in Athens in 450 is frankly unconvincing. Parmenides, who returned almost immediately, would not have had time to teach him anything, and Zeno, although he spent many years at the court of Pericles, associated with the Athenians at a time when relations between Samos and Athens were already soured.

Melissus only surfaces in history in 442 BC, the year marked by a skirmish between Samos and Miletus over the possession of Priene. Miletus came off worse in this neighbourhood squabble, but the day after the defeat her leaders immediately applied to Athens for the reinstatement of rights of which, they said, they had been unjustly deprived. We must remember that Athens, at that time, was regarded as a 'mother city' by all the other cities of the Aegean coast, so there was nothing unusual in this. Nevertheless, Plutarch[3] appears to think

[2]Diogenes Laertius, *op. cit.* IX 24.
[3]Plutarch, *Life of Pericles* XXV–XXVI.

that it was Pericles' mistress, Aspasia, rather than the Milesian delegation, who persuaded him to come to the defence of Miletus. Whatever the facts of the matter, the wretched Samians awoke one morning to find their island surrounded by a fleet of forty ships. The Athenian taskforce ousted the ruling party and replaced it with a democratic junta, then they took fifty hostages from among the sons of the most important families and installed a small garrison to safeguard their own interests. One group of the ruling body had managed to escape, however, and Melissus may well have been one of their number since, like most philosophers of the period, he was of aristocratic origin. The exiles found political asylum with Pissouthnes, tyrant of Sardis, and with his help they armed a band of seven hundred fighting men to retake possession of the conquered homeland. The expedition was a total success: the aristocrats regained control of the city and the occupying army was defeated. And in revenge for the Athenians having tattooed a Samian ship on the faces of several native aristocrats at the time of the invasion, the Samians now tattooed the faces of every Athenian with an owl, symbol of their coinage. Victory celebrations were not, however, unclouded: everyone knew that sooner or later Pericles would be back. They tried to mollify him by diplomacy and Pissouthnes even offered him ten thousand gold staters – and the venality of Pericles was a byword – but this time the injury had been too great, and he reluctantly refused. However, while the others parleyed, Melissus busied himself with defence measures, strengthening the walls and stocking the city with all the supplies he could lay his hands on.

The Athenians did not leave them long in suspense. Sixty ships under the command of Pericles himself first defeated the Samians in a naval battle and then beseiged the city on all sides. And this was the crisis in which Melissus covered himself with glory: taking advantage of a night when Pericles had withdrawn with a few of his triremes, he mounted a sortie and destroyed every remaining ship of the Athenian fleet. This heroic action saved a whitewash even though it failed to change the outcome of the war. Pericles in fact fitted out yet another fleet, even more powerful than the one before, and this time there was no escape for the Samians. The siege lasted for nine months and the city was eventually razed to the ground thanks to the new siege weapons invented by a certain Artemon Periphoretus. An Athenian architect, Periphoretus was a cripple and a homosexual and lived in such fear of accidents that he never left his house or even his chair, but remained constantly seated with two slaves standing beside him holding a shield over his head in case something fell on him.

Apart from being an able strategos, Melissus is known as the fourth philosopher of the Eleatic school. The chief difference between him and his predecessors is that whereas Parmenides defined *what is* as something outside time, Melissus identified it with empirical reality. 'What is was ever, and ever shall be',[4] he said, and this is where Aristotle took issue with him, outraged at his having downgraded Parmenides' One from the ideal to the matcrial.[5]

To us ordinary people the discrepancy between the two positions may seem minuscule, but a more careful assessment will soon show that it is, in fact, substantial.

Melissus is a practical man, or at least more so than Parmenides, if for no other reason than his sympathy with the physiologists of the Milesian school and Anaximander in particular. Thus, although he agrees with the Eleatics about the deceptiveness of appearances and the untrustworthiness of the senses, he refuses to accept that reality is empty and abstract but tries to endow it with a concrete quality and identifies it with the whole universe, that is, with something indeterminate and infinite which includes everything. Seen in this way, his reality is more nearly related to the *apeiron* of Anaximander than to the intangible One of Parmenides, although it has several points of similarity with the latter. Our naval commander states:[6]

• If something exists, it is eternal, since nothing can come from nothing.
• If it is eternal it is also infinite, because it has neither a beginning nor an end.
• If it is eternal and infinite it is one, because were it two, each would limit the other.
• If it is eternal, infinite and one, it is also homogeneous, because if

---

[4]Diels-Kranz, fr. 1
[5]Aristotle, *Metaphysics* I 5, 986b 25.
[6]Aristotle, *On Melissus, Gorgias and Xenophanes* 1– 2, 974a–977a.

it were not one part would be different from another and therefore a many.

- If it is eternal, infinite, one and homogeneous, it is also motionless, for there is nowhere outside itself for it to go.
- If it is eternal, infinite, one, homogeneous and motionless, it cannot suffer pain or grief, but must remain ever equal to itself.

Given that this is Melissus' theory and not some spurious rigmarole, we can lay comfort to our bosoms by noting the presence in the first sentence of the word 'exists'. This simplifying of reality enables us to find in the statements of Melissus a practical answer to our most anxious queries. Since each one of us is under the impression that something exists, it is comforting to know that reality is not only there but infinite, irrespective of earthly appearances.

So Melissus' reality is something good and positive. It is not yet an identikit picture of God, but it's not far off. From the concept of an infinite universe, one and eternal, to that of a God with the same characteristics, is a leap that becomes progressively smaller; and it is no chance that Melissus, in one of his statements, describes reality almost as if he were speaking of an old man with a beard: 'It cannot perish, nor become greater . . . for if it changed by so much as a single hair in ten thousand years, it would all perish in the whole of time.'[7]

[7]Diels-Kranz, fr. 7.

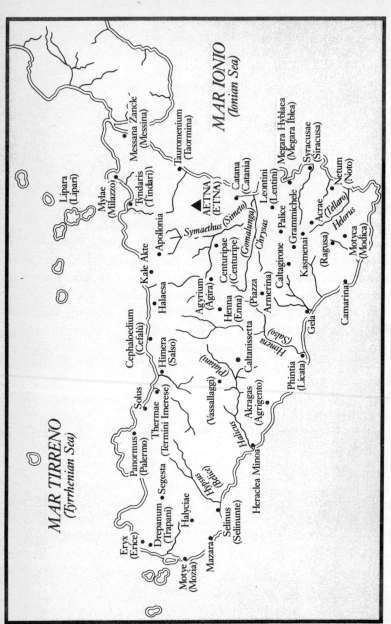

MAR TIRRENO
(Tyrrhenian Sea)

MAR IONIO
(Ionian Sea)

Lipara
(Lipari)

Messana Zancle
(Messina)

Mylae
(Milazzo)

Tyndaris
(Tindari)

Tauromenium
(Taormina)

Apollonia

Kale Akte

Catana
(Catania)

AETNA
(ETNA)

Symaethus (Simeto)

Leontini
(Lentini)

Megara Hyblaea
(Megara Iblea)

Syracusae
(Siracusa)

Halaesa

Centuripae
(Centuripe)

Gornalunga

Chrysas

Palice

Netum
(Noto)

Agyrium
(Agira)

Grammichele

Acrae

(Tellaro)

Helorus

Cephaloedium
(Cefalù)

Himera
(Salso)

Henna
(Enna)

Piazza
Armerina

Caltagirone

Kasmenai
(Ragusa)

Motyca
(Modica)

Solus

Thermae
(Termini Imerese)

Caltanissetta

(Platani)

Himera (Salso)

Phintia
(Licata)

Gela

Camarina

Panormus
(Palermo)

(Vassallaggi)

Akragas
(Agrigento)

Halicus

Heraclea Minoa

Hypsas (Belice)

Segesta

Thermae

Eryx
(Erice)

Drepanum
(Trapani)

Halyciae

Selinus
(Selinunte)

Mazara

Motye
(Mozia)

Fig. 5: **Ancient Sicily**

XV

Agrigento

rief history of Agrigento: One fine morning in the year 583 BC, a group of refugees from Rhodes and a thousand or so colonizers from nearby Gela under the command of Aristonous and Pistillus, decided to settle on a tract of land between two rivers, the Acragas and the Hypsas. The place seemed to fulfil all the requirements listed in the handbook for colonizers: to the East and West ran two clear, splendid rivers forming natural barriers for defence, to the North there was a craggy hill ideal for the siting of an Acropolis worthy of the name, and lastly the sea was no more than three kilometres away, near enough, that is, but not so near that one might wake up suddenly to find Carthaginians in the bedroom.

The colony grew rapidly, reaching two hundred thousand inhabitants in less than a hundred years.[1] When the tyrant Theron defeated the cities of Heraclea Minoa and Himera while Empedocles was still a lad, he carried away so many slaves that he was able to build dozens and dozens of exceedingly sumptuous public buildings. Today, a tourist visiting the Valley of the Temples will be struck above all by the Temple of Concord, the only one to survive whole; but if he pauses to reflect on the scattered remains of the Temple of Zeus Olympicus, he will realize immediately that he is looking at a gigantic construction: 110 by 55 metres is roughly the size of a football pitch,

---

[1]According to Timaeus, the colony had 800,000 inhabitants in the time of Empedocles (see Diogenes Laertius, *op. cit.* VIII 63). But given the space within the city walls, this seems unlikely.

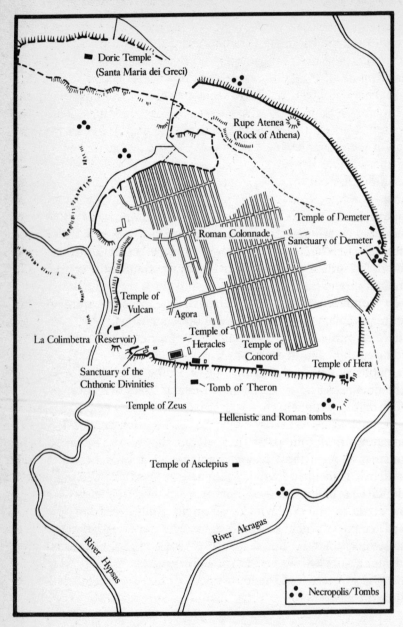

Fig. 6: **Agrigento**

but apply these same measurements to the perimeter walls of a temple, and the Parthenon itself pales by comparison.

So rich and so beautiful was Agrigento that Pindar called it 'loveliest of all mortal cities'. Even the cemeteries are reported to have been spectacular: apart from the chapels belonging to the aristocracy, embellished with bas-reliefs recording the deeds of the dead, there were also monuments to the memory of horses who had won at the Olympics. And even a sparrow, the sole playmate of an aristocratic girl, has his own mausoleum![2]

The statement that Agrigento enjoyed a better water supply in those days than it does now would, I believe, attract little by way of opposition. In the fifth century BC, in fact, it appears that the city boasted a communal aqueduct and a covered pool in which all the surplus water was collected. Today, on the other hand, rotas and water rationing are becoming ever more frequent during the summer months.

In commerce, too, the citizens of Agrigento were in the vanguard. They built a colossal emporium outside the city walls where they periodically staged the equivalent of a trade fair, attended by merchants from all around the Mediterranean. Tangible evidence of this trading superiority still survives in the very fine gold and silver coinage bearing the word 'Akragas' and the symbols of the city, the eagle, the quadriga or chariot, and the freshwater crab. Timaeus tells us that 'The Agrigentines live delicately as if tomorrow they would die, but they build their houses well as if they thought they would live for ever.'[3] A high standard of living was actually common to all the Sicilian cities. The Greeks looked on the island as an America *ante litteram*, a new world where one could make plenty of money without trying too hard. In the courts of the Sicilian tyrants there was an atmosphere that would later be called typical of the Renaissance. Domenico Scinà, an abbot who lived in the early nineteenth century, tells us that 'the two courts of Syracuse and Agrigento competed with each other in matters of courtly manners and elegance, rewarding

[2]D. Scinà, *Vita e filosofia d'Empedocle girgentino*, Palermo 1813, p. 52.
[3]Diogenes Laertius, *op. cit.* VIII 63.

outstanding talent and encouraging every excellent and useful skill.'[4]

When people are having a good time, spoilsports will always pop up and start to wag their heads. Diodorus grumbles that 'they had become so soft that during the Carthaginian siege an edict was promulgated forbidding the sentries to sleep with more than two pillows',[5] and Timaeus, an historian from Tauromenium and an incomparable gossip, presents us with the following description of an Agrigentine orgy of the fifth century BC: one evening, he says, there had been some very heavy drinking – and, I am tempted to add, possibly some drug taking – but anyway, when the banquet was in full swing, the guests began to imagine that, instead of being in a villa, they were on a ship being buffeted by the waves, so they became panic-stricken and started to throw all the furniture and tableware and ornaments out of the windows in a desperate attempt to lighten the ship and stay afloat for as long as possible. When the officers of law and order eventually arrived on the scene they were mistaken for marine deities and everyone threw themselves at their feet imploring forgiveness. From that day on, Timaeus adds, the house in question was nicknamed 'The Trireme'.[6]

Agrigento reached the peak of its glory at the beginning of the fifth century, first under the tyranny of Theron and then under the democracy which followed.

Theron was one of three great Sicilian tyrants who dominated the epoch; the other two, the brothers Gelon and Hieron, who ruled respectively in Syracuse and Gela, were related to him in a way since the former had married Theron's daughter. Faced with the threat of invasion from their Carthaginian neighbours and constant rebellions on the part of the Siceliots, these three gentlemen formed a strong military alliance, beating the Carthaginians definitively in a battle on the shores of the river Himera in 480, the very same year in which the Greeks destroyed the Persian fleet. According to Pindar, this was no coincidence, but a clear omen: *Zeus mit uns*, the Gods were on the side of the Greeks.[7]

[4]D. Scinà, *op. cit.* p. 28.
[5]Diodorus Siculus, XIII 84, 6.
[6]Athenaeus, *Deipnosophistae* II 37 B.
[7]Pindar, *Pyth.* I, vv. 75–81.

As is often the case, a generation of giants was succeeded by a generation of dwarfs: the heirs of Theron, Gelon and Hieron fell far short of their fathers' standards by squabbling among themselves and by underestimating the democratic opposition. Thrasydaeus, Theron's son, picked a quarrel with Syracuse and was given a sound drubbing; on his return he was exiled to Greece and there condemned to death. The democratic party in Agrigento was now in power; all the citizens who had compromised themselves with the old regime were purged and the alliance with Syracuse restored.

It was during this period of renewal that Empedocles, just twenty years old, stepped on to the stage of Agrigentine political life.

XVI
Empedocles

E mpedocles was a philosopher, a physician, a poet, a physicist and a democrat. Wrong: he was a medicine-man, a quack, a guru, one who claimed to be a god and thought he was superior to everyone else. What are we to believe? Who *was* Empedocles really? Perhaps the definition that comes nearest to the truth was Renan's: 'A man of multifarious skills, half Newton, half Cagliostro'.[1]

He was born in Agrigento in 492 BC into a wealthy and noble family. As with all the other Greek philosophers, the date of his birth is only approximate. His father's name was Meton and his grandfather was another Empedocles.[2] Grandfather Empedocles had, in fact, been the first member of the family to cover himself with glory: a horse-breeder, he won a race at the 71st Olympiad and became famous throughout the Panhellenic world. I should explain that an Olympic victory in those days was considered an event of quite exceptional importance: the winners were wined and dined in style by the chief magistrates and their names inscribed on the civic rolls of honour. When Diagoras, himself an Olympic victor, saw both his sons victors too, other spectators invited him to commit suicide on the spot: 'Kill yourself, Diagoras,' they said, 'for life can offer you no more than this!'[3] Empedocles senior celebrated his win rather more

[1]E. Renan, *Vingt jours en Sicilie. Mélanges d'histoire et de voyages*, p. 103.
[2]Diogenes Laertius, *op. cit.* VIII 51.
[3]For information about Diagoras, see article by F. Jacoby: *Diagoras ho atheos* in 'Abhandlungen der deutschen Akademie der Wissenschaften', Berlin, 1959.

prudently by feasting his fellow-citizens on a confection of honey and barley-meal fashioned into the shape of an ox.[4]

Empedocles was not yet sixteen when he heard Xenophanes speak in the colonnades of the Temple of Hercules. After the lesson, he asked the master if there were some way of recognizing a wise man, and the old philosopher replied that there was nothing difficult about this – as long as one was a wise man oneself.[5] The boy probably did not understand all the ideas taught by the nonagenarian teacher from Colophon, but this, nevertheless, was the moment when he decided to dedicate himself to the study of nature.

After a brief but intensive period of political militancy, during which he helped to overthrow the regime of Theron's son Thrasydeus, he went to Elea. He was probably hoping to see Xenophanes again, but encountered Zeno and Parmenides instead. The visit was a failure. One can well imagine the young Empedocles, fresh from his involvement in the Agrigentine conflict of '72, as a man of action, eager to come to grips with the world. Parmenides' abstract intellectualism must have seemed totally divorced from reality.[6]

'Bored with these subtleties',[7] he returned to Sicily and enrolled himself in the school of Pythagoras. Opinions vary as to who was his teacher (Pythagoras' son Telauges? Brontinus? Epicharmus?) but we do know that he was soon in trouble with the Pythagoreans too. As we have already seen, the school was more of a politico-religious sect than an institute of learning, and Empedocles, with his extrovert character, was anything but a model pupil. Accused of 'stealing discourses' and flouting the Pythagorean rule by telling tales out of school, he was demoted to the group which was not allowed to speak during lectures. Not such a disgrace if one remembers that the same treatment was later meted out to Plato.[8]

Of all the subjects taught at the Pythagorean school, those that appealed most to Empedocles were Magic and Metempsychosis. Even so, he suspected a reluctance on the part of his masters to

[4]Diogenes Laertius, *op. cit.* VIII 53.
[5]Diogenes Laertius, *op. cit.* IX 20.
[6]E. Bignone, *Empedocle*, Turin 1916, p. 74.
[7]D. Scinà, *op. cit.*, p. 32.
[8]Diogenes Laertius, *op. cit.* VIII 55.

divulge the mysteries fully, so he decided to bypass them and go straight to the source, the oriental schools which were the universities of his day. From the Egyptians, the Chaldeans and above all the Magi, he learned the mystic arts of hypnosis, telekinesis and thought-reading. Pliny and other historians later treated him as a charlatan on account of his esoteric practices, but in so doing they were consciously turning a blind eye to the fact that the practice of magic was then considered an eminently respectable profession. Men wanted mediators between themselves and the gods, and for this they resorted to magicians, regarding them as a race of lesser deities. The cult was called Theurgy. Another religious cult arose later among the Chaldeans whose adepts, the Goetics, practised black rites, meeting in dark caves and offering human sacrifices. The two cults eventually became confused in people's minds and the reputation of the Magi suffered in consequence. It is important to remember, however, that Empedocles was also an excellent physician within the limits imposed by his times. His contemporaries, for example, considered him an expert on human anatomy. Medicine in the early fifth century was largely the province of the philosophers and was dominated by religion. It was popularly believed that rapid cures could be effected by 'stimulating the imagination of the patient'.[9] Only later, with Hippocrates, did medicine become a science in its own right.

Returning to his homeland, Empedocles set about moral reforms. He found that standards both of public and private morality had dropped and advocated that his fellow-citizens should 'fast from wickedness' to purge themselves of their wrongdoing. Accusing the administrators of having robbed the public purse, he broke up the assembly of One Thousand[10] (the group of aristocrats who had managed to insinuate themselves once more into positions of power) and put forward the idea of a new government based upon civil equality. Such was the public enthusiasm for these schemes that he was offered the kingship. This the philosopher naturally refused[11] (as Heraclitus had done before), but we have every reason to assume that

---

[9]D. Scinà, *op. cit.*, p. 86.
[10]Diogenes Laertius, *op. cit.* VIII 66.
[11]Diogenes Laertius, *op. cit.* VIII 63.

had they offered the title of God he might well have accepted.

He liked to walk around the streets of Agrigento preceded by a crowd of young men and surrounded by servants and admirers. He affected a purple robe, a golden girdle and slippers of bronze. His hair and beard were luxuriant and upon his head he wore a Delphic laurel-wreath in honour of Apollo. This is how he described himself:

O friends, you that inhabit the city on the yellow rock of Akragas, up by the citadel, . . . all hail. I go about among you an immortal god, no longer mortal, honoured by all as is meet, girdled with bands and crowned with flowery garlands. When I enter into the flourishing cities, both by men and by women am I honoured; they follow me in their thousands, asking of me what is the way to gain; some desire oracles, others, afflicted by every kind of disease, beg to hear from me the word of healing. (fr. 112)[12]

This self-portrait is strangely uncontemporary in feeling and tends to make us associate Empedocles, who was actually the contemporary of Socrates and Democritus, more with the age of Pythagoras.

Empedocles was both a scientist and a prophet. When the town of Selinus was ravaged by an epidemic, he realized that the pestilence originated in a ditch of foul water that ran through the heart of the town, so, having examined the surrounding territory carefully, he ordered trenches to be dug – at his own expense – to bring water from other sources into the ditch so that instead of being stagnant, the water would flow even in periods of drought.[13] I hardly need add that after this intervention he was regarded as a god by the inhabitants of Selinus too.

On another occasion, he prevented the sirocco devastating crops in a valley near Agrigento by blocking a narrow gorge with hundreds of bags made from the skins of flayed mules. Once again a public calamity had been averted by his ingenuity. Whatever the truth of

[12]Fragments are given according to the order of Diels-Kranz and quoted with reference to Burnet, *op. cit.*, p. 199ff.
[13]Diogenes Laertius, *op. cit.* VIII 70.

this anecdote, he was henceforth dubbed the 'wind-stayer'.[14]

Aristotle called him the 'inventor of Rhetoric'.[15] Gorgias and Pausanias took lessons from him, and this gave rise to the usual accusations of homosexuality, specifically on the part of Aristippus and Satyrus,[16] but I should hope that my reader has by now become accustomed to the sexual proclivities of the philosophers.

Empedocles was well able to make himself pleasant in company but was a stickler when it came to principles. Once, when he was a guest at a banquet, he wondered at the fact that his host had offered nothing to drink. He called for wine and was told that none would be served until a certain political personage had arrived. And so it was: as soon as this man made his appearance, the host drank a toast to him and named him 'symposiarch', king of the revels. The philosopher was seriously displeased, and in the senate next day he accused the two friends of plotting a tyranny and had them condemned to death.[17] For half an hour without wine, I call that verdict excessive.

He wrote two poems in hexameters, *On Nature* and *Purifications*, of which only 400 verses have survived out of the original 5,000. Aristotle states that he also wrote forty-three tragedies, some political tracts, an historical account of Xerxes and a hymn to Apollo, but that he came to despise these works as unworthy of his genius and ordered his sister to burn them all in one go.[18] Empedocles remains, however, one of the best of the philosopher–poets. He was also a good singer, apparently, for one day when he was the guest of the judge Anchitus, a young man burst into the house and attacked the magistrate for having condemned his father to death the very same day, whereupon Empedocles, showing extraordinary perception, seized a lyre that happened to be to hand and with perfect sang-froid began to sing:

> *Here is a salve for wrath and pain,*
> *this brings oblivion of all ills.*

[14] Diogenes Laertius. *op. cit.* VIII, 60 (See also Plutarch, *De curiositate* 1, 515 C.)
[15] Aristotle, fr. 65 Rose. (See also Diog. VIII 57.)
[16] Diogenes Laertius, *op. cit.* VIII 60.
[17] Diogenes Laertius, *op. cit.* VIII 64.
[18] Aristotle, fr. 70 Rose. (See also Diog. VIII 57.)

To cut a long story short, the youth calmed down at once and Empedocles had saved the life of his friend. As for the attacker, he became one of the philosopher's best disciples.[19] Of the many miracles attributed to Empedocles, I shall mention only that of his healing a woman who had been in a coma for thirty days, quoting the version given by the Abbot Scinà: 'A woman in Agrigento was suffering from a uterine illness of the kind termed *hysterical* by masters of medicine; there is no doubt that among women especially, many have been known to feign, but in the case of the woman from Agrigento it would seem the illness was genuine, because she was incapable of feeling any sensation, her breathing had stopped, and everyone was convinced that she was dead. But Empedocles took her by the hand and restored her to life.'[20]

When we come to the manner of Empedocles' death we are spoiled for choice: there are no less than six separate versions of this event and almost all contain an element of the spectacular. Apart from Scinà's version, which reports self-strangulation (?) at the age of sixty, all are faithfully recorded by Diogenes:[21] Timaeus claimed he died from natural causes after being exiled to the Peloponnese; Demetrius of Troezen asserted that he hanged himself from the branch of a cornel tree; Neanthes of Cyzicus related that he met his death at the age of seventy-seven by falling from a carriage while on his way to a popular festival in Messina; Telauges, in a letter to his friend Philolaus, said that he fell, being very old and weak, into the sea. The most famous version, and the one which seems most in keeping with his personality, is that given by Heraclides of Pontus who said that immediately after curing the woman in a coma, Empedocles, realizing that his fame was at its peak, decided that the only thing he could now do was disappear like a god. He accordingly threw himself into the crater of Etna, an action that was confirmed moments later by the volcano belching out one of his famous bronze slippers.[22] Unfortunately this version is somewhat undermined, partly by the dictates of common sense, partly by the distance between Agrigento and

---

[19]Iamblichus, *Life of Pythagoras* 113.
[20]D. Scinà, *op. cit.*, p. 89.
[21]Diogenes Laertius, *op. cit.* VIII 71–74.
[22]Heraclides of Pontus, fr. 83 Wehrli.

Mount Etna and also by the scant credibility of Heraclides himself, who insisted elsewhere that he had spoken to a man who had fallen from the moon.[23]

As we have said already, besides being a magician, Empedocles was also a scientist, a philosopher and a poet.

As a man of science, his major contribution was the discovery of the existence of Air as a substance, recognizably identical with the one we generally refer to as Air, and completely distinct from the void. In a fragment of his poem *On Nature*, the Agrigentine philosopher says that 'if a girl, playing with a water-clock[24] of shining brass, closes the orifice of the neck with her comely hand and then dips the vessel into the yielding mass of silvery water, the stream does not then flow into the vessel, but the bulk of the air inside keeps it out.' (fr. 100)[25] He soon discovered centrifugal force, too, noting that if we tie a piece of string to the handle of a bucket containing water and then whirl the bucket round in a circle, the water sticks to the bottom of the bucket and does not escape; and he eventually enunciated a primitive but striking form of the theory of evolution, anticipating the revolutionary theories of Darwin by two thousand three hundred years.

According to this theory, particles of the primordial elements combined without any prearranged order and the first living creatures were born quite by chance. 'Heads sprang up without necks, arms wandered bare and bereft of shoulders, eyes strayed up and down in want of foreheads' (fr. 57), there were 'shambling creatures with countless hands' (fr. 60), and 'many creatures were born with faces and breasts looking in different directions; some, offspring of oxen with the faces of men, while others, again, arose as offspring of men with the heads of oxen' (fr. 61). There was, in other words, a world of monsters whose various parts had been assembled by no guiding intelligence but, quite on the contrary, in the most chaotic and haphazard way. Only a Bosch or a Jacovitti would be capable of depicting a world like this.

[23]Heraclides of Pontus, fr. 84 Wehrli.
[24]This was the *klepsydra*, a metal vessel having a narrow neck at the top and a sort of strainer pierced with holes at the bottom. Burnet, *op. cit.*, p. 219.
[25]The fragments are numbered according to Diels-Kranz.

As time passed, however, the most ill-assorted of the mixtures began to die off and the only creatures to survive were those whose parts were 'mingled with divinity' (fr. 59).

Empedocles' philosophy serves as a summary of much that had gone before: he possessed the naturalistic vision of the Milesian school, shared many of the Pythagoreans' mystic beliefs and united once and for all the Being of Parmenides with the Becoming of Heraclitus.

Empedocles shared a favourite theme with the Ionian philosophers, that of a cosmogony, and has left us some extremely beautiful lines on the subject:

> *Hear first the four roots of all things:*
> *shining Zeus, life-bringing Hera,*
> *Aidoneius and Nestus whose tear-drops*
> *are a well-spring for mortals.*

In plain language, he is saying that there are four primordial elements in nature: Fire, Air, Earth and Water. Their intermingling is brought about by the intervention of two things, two active principles which Empedocles calls Love and Strife.

In the beginning, we are told, Love reigned supreme, and hence 'all things that are more adapted for mixture are like to one another and united in love by Aphrodite' (fr. 22). Empedocles defines the world in this first phase as 'the Sphere', perhaps in homage to the Spherical Being of Parmenides. Within the Sphere is nothing but harmony and joy: 'There [in the Sphere] are distinguished neither the swift limbs of the sun, no, nor the shaggy earth in its might, nor the sea – so fast was the god bound in the close covering of Harmony, spherical and round, rejoicing in his circular solitude' (fr. 27). But Strife managed to infiltrate this perfection, thereby giving rise to the second phase, which is, if I am not much mistaken, the one in which we currently find ourselves.

If we are to believe Empedocles, Strife is due to gain the upper hand at some point and cause the destruction of the world (Good grief: yet another prophecy of an atomic apocalypse!) but, in the fourth phase, Love will return.

To sum up: Love and Strife are two cooks who have only four jars of ingredients from which to concoct their dainty dishes. Anything can happen in the kitchen of the Sphere: sometimes Love will reign and all will be sweetness and light, at other times Strife will dominate and all be as silent as the tomb. At other times both cooks are present simultaneously and the result is a slapstick comedy of the custard-pie-in-the-face variety. These, I contend, are the best, or at least the most entertaining, of times.

If we read the surviving fragments of *On Nature* carefully, we notice that Empedocles' theories are not as simple as they might appear at first glance. For example, there is one place where he writes: 'I shall tell thee a twofold tale. At one time the one grew out of the many; at another the one divided anew to become many. There is a double becoming of perishable things and a double passing away' (fr. 17). In his use of the word *one*, Empedocles is evidently taking his cue from Parmenides' theory of the One which is unique and immovable, but when he refers to the *many*, it is Heraclitus' concept of Becoming which pops up again. In fact, Empedocles' four primordial roots possess the immobility of the Parmenidian Being and, despite being four, also all the attributes of the One; but by their mixing and separating they provide us with an explanation of Becoming and Plurality. Every birth is also a death because, while on the one hand it gives rise to a new 'mingling', on the other it dissolves something which previously existed in another form. In putting forward such ideas, he demythologizes the concepts of birth and death and replaces them with the less dramatic images of 'mingling and interchange' (fr. 8).

The breakdown of the four elements into minute particles that can intermingle foreshadows to some extent the atomic theories of Leucippus and Democritus. Unlike them, however, Empedocles does not admit the existence of the void, substantiating his view by saying that 'nothing can arise from what in no way is' (fr. 12). This expression, found in the works of so many of the pre-Socratic philosophers, is the basis of Greek atheism. If you are convinced that nothing can arise from nothing, you do, in fact, negate the concept of creation and must accept one of three theories: an eternal and immovable entity (Parmenides), a universe in continual change

(Heraclitus), or a combination of the two (Empedocles). None of these three, however, allows for the intervention of a Superior Being, the divine spark that sets everything in motion. The Greeks believed in their gods and sacrificed to them, but these gods were not creators of heaven and earth, rather types of Superman, objects of worship superendowed in comparison with ordinary mortals but themselves subject to the dictates of Fate.

Empedocles has often been accused of one particular inconsistency. In many places in his poem, *On Nature*, he states that Love unites and Strife divides, while at other times he maintains that Love tends to unite like with like and that the greater the affinity between two particles of matter, the greater will be their reciprocal love. If, says Empedocles, we take a stone, a bucket of water and some smoke and turn them loose to go wherever they will, we see that the stone will be attracted to the earth, the water will tend to seek out the sea and the smoke will rise to the sky. These observations were queried by Aristotle, however, when he said: 'If a man pays heed to reason, he realizes that Love is the efficient cause of Good, and Strife the efficient cause of Evil, but if he were to heed the babblings of Empedocles, according to which everything tends to unite with something similar to itself, he would soon descend into an uninhabitable world where each of the four elements lay inert and separate.'[26] In other words, Aristotle regarded Love as a positive force which could never, in any instance, be responsible for such a disastrously negative result as the separating-out of the primordial elements.

Empedocles' views on religion were those of a practising Pythagorean. He hated beans, avoided eating the flesh of animals and believed in metempsychosis. He declared himself to have been 'a boy and a girl, a bush and a bird and a dumb fish in the sea' (fr. 117). He believed in the existence of demons who 'by an ancient ordinance of the gods, eternal and sealed fast by broad oaths, having sinfully polluted their hands with blood, or followed strife and forsworn themselves, must wander thrice ten thousand seasons from the abodes of the blessed, being born throughout the time in all manners of mortal forms, changing one toilsome path of life for another. For

[26]Aristotle, *Metaphysics* I 4, 984b 32.

the mighty Air drives them into the sea, and the sea spews them forth on the dry Earth; Earth tosses them into the beams of the blazing Sun, and he flings them back to the eddies of Air. One takes them from the other, and all reject them. One of these – concludes the philosopher – I now am, an exile and a wanderer from the gods, for that I put my trust in insensate strife' (fr. 115).[27]

Empedocles is the most poetic of all the poet-philosophers of his time. *On Nature* purports, in the final analysis, to be no more than a treatise on the natural sciences, yet even here, whenever Empedocles speaks of a heavenly body, a meteorological phenomenon or a human being, he does so with a wealth of splendid imagery that reveals the power of his creative genius.

Here are some samples: 'The sharp-darting sun' (fr. 40), 'the pale-faced moon' (fr. 42), 'Sea, the sweat of the earth' (fr. 55), 'solitary, blind-eyed night' (fr. 49). And when his subject is parturition and he has to indicate the place from which the baby makes his début, he conjures up a most striking metaphor: 'The divided meadows of Aphrodite' (fr. 66).

---

[27]See also Hippolytus, *Refutation of all Heresies* VII 29.

XVII
Gennaro Bellavista

he intrusion of Professor Bellavista,[1] a retired schoolteacher, into the history of Greek philosophy is justified by the fact that his ideas stand in direct relation to the cosmogony of Empedocles and the ethic of Epicurus. That said, we can deal straight away with the first topic, that of the structure of the universe, but we shall reserve our description of the Neapolitan character, or rather the Neapolitan ethic, for another volume and deal with it in the context of the school of Epicurus.

According to Bellavista, the *archè*, the primordial stuff of which the world was made, is Energy. This is worked upon by two active principles which the Professor calls Love and Liberty. In contrast to Empedocles' Love and Strife, the Bellavistine forces, although mutually inimical, turn out to be both positive and therefore life enhancing. Aristotle's principal objection to the theories of Empedocles, that the workings of Love would eventually prove negative, therefore does not apply.

Energy, Bellavista maintains, is found in two distinct forms in nature, as Matter or as Explosive Force, depending upon whether the binding forces between protons and neutrons within the atom are principally governed by Love or Liberty.

With this in mind, I think it might be useful to brush up on some elementary astronomy before looking at Bellavista's

[1]For a more exhaustive account of the theories of Love and Liberty, the reader is referred to *Thus Spake Bellavista*.

theories in detail. In the year 1596 a star was discovered whose behaviour was quite extraordinary: at times it shone with exceeding brightness and at others it paled to the point of invisibility. This star belonged to the constellation of the Whale or Cetus (in the southern hemisphere), 163 light-years away from the earth. The discovery created such a furore that the star was christened Mira, 'the Marvel'. There are now known to be 4566 stars like Mira Ceti and they are known as the 'cepheid variables'; each has its own period of variability during which its volume (and hence its luminosity) changes. The period of Mira, for example, is 331 days.

The variability of the cepheids coincides with the continual contraction and expansion of their constituent gases. When the mass contracts the internal temperature rises violently to a point just short of explosion, while dilation produces a cooling effect and prepares the next phase of contraction. The star is pre-set, as it were, to oscillate between two boundaries, one of minimum and one of maximum density. Sometimes, however, this balance is upset, and then the star either explodes like a gigantic hydrogen bomb or contracts into a nucleus of unimaginable density. When the former happens the result is a *nova* (or a *supernova* in the case of a giant star), so called because of the apparent birth of a star in a part of the sky previously deemed empty; when the latter occurs, on the other hand, a so-called *black hole* is created, in which the force of gravity reaches such an intensity that nothing can escape, not even light.

Now, asking himself what the forces could be that cause matter to expand or contract, Bellavista formulated the hypothesis that the entire universe is regulated by the centripetal and centrifugal forces of Love and Liberty. In other words, protons and neutrons are at the mercy of two exceedingly powerful drives which act simultaneously upon them, one compelling them to stick together, the other compelling them to escape outwards. We know that every object, an ashtray, for example, is nothing but a mass of millions and millions of atoms compressed into a small space; so, should the binding forces within the nucleus break up, even our humble ashtray would release enough energy to make the bomb dropped on Hiroshima pale by comparison. All matter, then, is full of energy that will remain in a dormant stage until an event occurs capable of activating it. With the famous formula $E=mc^2$, all Einstein did was to demonstrate the existence of a proportion between the mass 'm' of the ashtray and the energy 'E' it would emit.

The most widely accepted theory about the origin of the universe is undoubtedly that of the 'Big Bang', first put forward by Abbé Lemaître. According to this theory, when time began (a dubious expression in itself!) the entire cosmos consisted of a single mass of highly compressed matter sometimes called Ylem (by whom?) whose internal temperature and specific weight were of wellnigh infinite proportions. At a certain point, Lemaître maintains, this mass exploded and the universe started to expand. But we must be careful to define our terms here, because by 'explosion' in this context we are not implying a blast that starts from a specific centre and moves outwards, but one in which every particle suddenly moves away from every other particle, creating, in effect, a simultaneous explosion of every point in space.

Like Empedocles, Bellavista is convinced that when time began Love was the single dominating factor and that Liberty prowled around waiting for the right moment to catch it unawares and split the binding elements within the mass. Subjected to these two tremendous forces, the mass was compelled to pulsate like any variable star until it eventually exploded at all points: Liberty had brought about the disintegration of Love. The Big Bang is supposed to have taken place twenty-five billion years ago, and the explosion is still in progress. If we look at the firmament through a spectroscope, we can see that this is indeed the case, and that the galaxies are still moving away from a hypothetical centre. Astronomers describe this more correctly as an expanding universe.

The conflict between Love and Liberty which is inherent in matter is also present in human mentality. Each one of us, according to Bellavista, is subject to two opposing drives: a great impulse to Love, which causes us to seek the companionship of our fellows, and an irresistible desire to defend our own privacy. There is no stability in this condition, however, because there are times when we suffer from loneliness and others when we feel suffocated by the proximity of other people. If we find ourselves sitting in a traffic jam, for instance, we begin to feel a certain hostility towards other drivers, but if we have been sailing alone on the open sea for some time and another vessel appears on the horizon, we are immediately prepared to hail perfect strangers with affection.

Bellavista defines individuals dominated by one or other of these impulses as 'men of Love' or 'men of Liberty'. Nations, too, can be similarly classified. The English, the inventors of privacy (no analogous word exists in the Italian language), are obviously a people of Liberty; the Neapolitans, *anema e core*,[2] fall inevitably into the category of Love.

The novelty of Bellavista's theory is that, translated into a Cartesian co-ordinate system, Love and Liberty are seen not as standing in opposition to each other, but as bisecting each other at right angles and positive in both cases. In other words, if we draw two Cartesian axes and define the abscissa and the ordinate as Love and Liberty respectively, we can plot a position for every human being, represented by a P, relative to two co-ordinates that will show in what proportion the person in question needs to love or to be free.

It is vital that we should be aware of our own position on the Cartesian diagram because only by an exact evaluation of our own tendencies can we possibly make the right choices in our lives. The man of Love, for example, can only be happy if he has someone to love him, because he needs love as a plant needs water: it is an essential requirement for life itself. The man of Liberty, on the other hand, regards the space around him as sacrosanct and cannot achieve even a minimal level of serenity if

[2] *Translator's note*: 'Heart and soul', the words of one of the best loved of all Neapolitan songs.

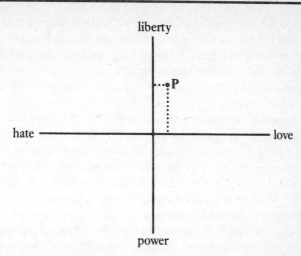

he feels it to be threatened. Liberty for him means air, wide open spaces, the need for change.

If we look again at the Cartesian axes, we see that they divide the plan into quadrants, each of which has a particular significance.

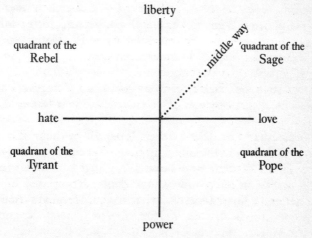

The first quadrant, that of the 'Sage', is where we find the best kind of people, those who cultivate within themselves the impulses of Love and Liberty simultaneously. Among these, the wisest are those who achieve a reasonable balance between the dictates of the head and the heart. They will be found nearest to the 'middle way' and are those capable of loving without making demands. If you are fortunate enough to encounter a specimen of this type, hang on to it for dear life!

The second quadrant is that of the 'Pope', defined as the combination of Love and Power. Here we find a great number of women, all the wives and mothers who love possessively, and also, naturally, men of the jealous type and those old-fashioned industrialists who are simultaneously open hearted and close fisted in dealing with their employees. We give the name of 'Pope' to this quadrant because Love and Power are the proper prerogatives of the Holy See. Even so, by no means every pope in history would find a place here: John Paul II would, but not John XXIII, whose place is with the sages (nearer the axis of Love than that of Liberty, of course). And there are the awkward popes, too, such as Alexander VI and Boniface VIII, men totally unscrupulous yet wielding enormous power, whom Bellavista unhesitatingly consigns to the next quadrant, that of the 'Tyrant'. In this sector, Hate and Power define the area in which the worst people find their niche. For the occupants of the middle line in this category we can choose between Hitler, Stalin and Caligula: one is much the same as another. Certainly not the Devil: as pure Hate, he occupies the extreme point on his half of the abscissa as of right; nor can we place Mussolini there because, as the founder of Fascism, he holds a fair rating of Power.

The last quadrant, that of the 'Rebel', is perhaps the most ambiguous thanks to the intermingling of such apparently antithetical forces as Hate and Love, but imagine yourself in the shoes of a fedayee and you will soon realize how Hate and Love can combine to form an explosive mixture. Wherever dictatorship exists there is also a thirst for Liberty, hence Hate and the urge to revolt. So between one extreme and the other of this fourth quadrant we find every shade of revolutionary, from the members of the Red or Black Brigades to the anarchic idealist dreaming of a free and happy land. Every time Bellavista happens to witness a march or demonstration, he searches the faces of the participants for signs of this or that emotion.

Before leaving our sketch of Bellavista's theory, we should make it clear that the point representing an individual is far from stationary; it varies according to the prevailing conditions. If we are abandoned by a loved one or suffer an injustice or if a friend lands himself on us for more than two weeks, we soon find point P making considerable excursions into strange territory. Even so, there will always be an area which, allowing for a comfortable degree of mobility, becomes an identifiably personal zone because it embraces our most frequent moods.

We should also point out that the Bellavista theory aspires to be no more than an attempt to analyse behaviour in terms of geometry. Obviously, the human psyche cannot be reduced to only two impulses, Love and Liberty, however predominant these may be; however, if we were to represent the human soul in a conceptual, rather than a graphical form, and to replace two-dimensional space by a space having n dimensions where n stood for all the variables that influence personality, Bellavista's theory would still be valid. In this case envy, competitiveness, sex, greed and every other driving force would each have its own axis and play a part in determining the eventual position of point P.

Finally, following on from this idea of space having n dimensions, Bellavista has a stab at describing God in geometrical terms. If we attribute to God the maximum degree of every human capacity (hence omnipotent, omniscient and so on), the point that represents him will consist of an infinite extension of every line on the axes, or what geometricians call an 'ideal plane'. In rather simpler words, every straight line can be extended or produced to infinity, and this imaginary point is defined as 'ideal'; collectively, these ideal points are referred to as an 'ideal plane', which, if you think of it, must resemble not so much a plane as a sphere with an infinite number of rays. And if we carry the analogy a step further, even the figure of a sphere becomes inadequate, since we have already described space as having n dimensions.

Fig. 7: **The Graeco-Persian Wars**

XVIII
Athens in the Fifth Century

et's leave philosophy alone for a moment and glance at history. Humanity can be amazing at times: a millenium can pass in which nothing happens at all, then suddenly, in less than a hundred years and within little more than one square mile, everything happens at once! I refer, of course, to Athens in the fifth century BC.

Even to jot down, quite haphazardly, a list of names connected with this period leaves us somewhat breathless. Among those born in Athens, immigrants to the city and visiting intellectuals we find the philosophers Anaxagoras, Gorgias, Protagoras, Parmenides, Zeno, Melissus, Democritus, Archelaus, Socrates, Plato, Hippias, Prodicus, Isocrates and Antiphon, the tragic dramatists Aeschylus, Sophocles and Euripides, the comic dramatist Aristophanes, the physician Hippocrates, the artists Myron, Phidias, Praxiteles, Zeuxis, Ictinus, Hippodamus, Callicrates, Mnesicles, Alcamenes, Cresilas and Polyclitus, the historians Herodotus, Thucydides and Xenophon, the orators Hypereides, Thrasymachus and Lysias, and finally, the statesmen Themistocles, Miltiades, Cimon, Pericles, Aristides and Alcibiades. As Bertrand Russell says: 'It was possible in that age, as in few others, to be both intelligent and happy, and happy through intelligence.'[1]

The fifth century began with a revolt, that of the Ionians against the Persians; the Ionian who started it was a certain Aristagoras, governor

[1]Bertrand Russell, *op. cit.*, p. 77.

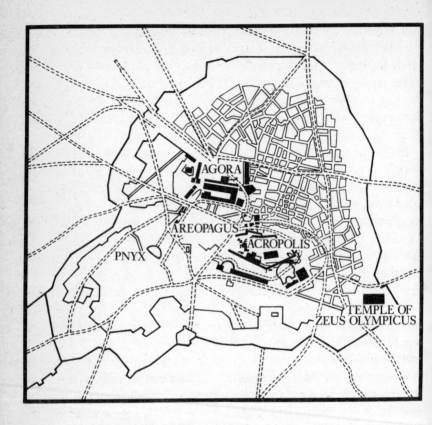

Fig. 8: **Athens: The city in the fifth century** BC

of Miletus. The strangest anecdote about the beginning of the Persian Wars concerns Histiaeus, the man who planned the revolt. To get his message about the date and time for the start of operations safely through to Aristagoras, he shaved the head of a deaf and dumb slave, tattooed the message on his scalp and then, having waited for the hair to grow again, sent him off to Miletus, safe in the knowledge that even if the slave were caught, the message would never be intercepted.[2]

In the event, the peoples of the coast rose as one man and the Persian army of occupation was defeated throughout the land. But in spite of their success the rebels were uneasy, knowing that sooner or later Darius would return with an even larger army than the one that had conquered Ionia to begin with. With this eventuality in mind, the Milesian governor Aristagoras went to the Greek mainland in the autumn of 499 and tried to persuade the most important cities to join together in a grand alliance that would unite all the Greeks on both sides of the Aegean. Sparta refused point-blank: Persia was too far away for them to feel involved. The enmity of the Thebans was directed exclusively at Athens and for this, if for no other reason, she would never join a coalition. The Greeks, in short, found a quarrel with their neighbours much more stimulating than a hypothetical invasion from outside. Aristagoras only succeeded with Erythrea and Athens, who agreed by common consent to furnish twenty ships. This gesture of solidarity was, in Herodotus' words, the *archè kakòn*, the beginning of trouble, for Greeks and Persians alike.[3]

As soon as the decision to fight had been taken, the Ionians and Athenians set sail for Miletus, but instead of lying low behind the walls of the city and waiting for the Persians to come to them, they decided to strike first and marched inland to Anatolia. Sardis was first to suffer. Herodotus tells us that no sooner was it captured than a soldier set a house alight and in the course of one night the entire city, including the temples, was destroyed by fire.

When the Persian king Darius heard about this he was furious: 'Who destroyed Sardis?'

---

[2]Herodotus, *op. cit.* V 35.
[3]Herodotus, *op. cit.* V 97.

'The Ionians and Athenians.'

'The Ionians and who?' Darius asked, never having heard the name before.

'The Athenians.'

Then the king of kings called for his bow, fired an arrow into the air and cried:

'Grant, O God, that I may punish the Athenians!'

After which he commanded one of his servants to repeat the following phrase to him every time he sat down to dinner: 'Master, remember the Athenians!'[4] So, with the words of this memo ringing in his ears after hearing them three times a day, once before every meal, good King Darius set out upon the invasion of Greece in 490.

An enormous fleet of six hundred ships, each one laden to capacity with soldiers and horses, crossed the Aegean from Samos. Erythrea was besieged and destroyed, its temples burnt in revenge for the outrage perpetrated in Sardis. Athens appealed to Sparta for help, but the Spartans replied that their law forbade them to take the field until the moon was full; after the ninth by all means, but for the moment their hands were tied.[5] So the only support came from the Plataeans, and from that day on they were remembered with honour by the Athenians at every festival.

The battle took place on the plain of Marathon (490). Miltiades, elected as leading strategos by the drawing of lots, deployed the strongest forces on the wings, thus deliberately weakening the centre; the Persians naturally attacked the weak point, broke through and were immediately surrounded and cut down. According to Herodotus,[6] 6,400 barbarians were killed and 192 Athenians. On the subject of these figures, however, we beg leave to assume that the historian's loyalty to his own side may have run away with him. True to their word, the Spartans turned up after the full moon. The battle was over by then so the strong Lacedaemonians could do nothing except satisfy their curiosity by looking at the bodies of the dead Persians and compliment the Athenians on a good job.

[4]Herodotus, *op. cit.* V 105.
[5]Herodotus, *op. cit.* VI 106.
[6]Herodotus, *op. cit.* VI 117.

Flushed with success, the Athenians were convinced that the danger from Asia was now over. Not so the wily Themistocles: the Athenian archon immediately set about the organization of a great Hellenic alliance. Every Greek city was obliged to contribute to the general cause by providing ships or money, and as most of them opted for money, Athens was able to turn it to her own advantage and become the strongest military power.

In the meantime, Darius had died and his son Xerxes now ruled the Persian Empire. After a period of hesitation, Xerxes also decided to take the plunge. Anxious to avoid repeating his father's mistakes, he did things on the grand scale and marched upon Greece with an army the like of which had never been seen before. According to the reports, it comprised 1,700,000 foot soldiers and 80,000 horsemen.[7] 'Save for the great rivers,' says Herodotus, 'there was not a stream his army drank from that was not drunk dry.'[8]

The attack was two pronged: by land, passing through Thrace, Macedonia and Thessaly, and by sea, with a fleet of 1200 ships. The first problem for the land forces was to cross the straits of the Dardanelles. A tempest having destroyed the wooden bridge built by the Egyptian engineers, Xerxes commanded that the waters of the Hellespont should be punished with 300 strokes of the whip[9] while he uttered the words, 'You salt and bitter stream, your master lays this punishment upon you for injuring him, who never injured you. But Xerxes the king will cross you, with or without your permission,' after which he had his engineers lash 300 ships together to form a pontoon and crossed into Europe with his army. The crossing took seven days and seven nights without a break. Every race within the empire was to be found in the army: Medes, Cissians, Hyrcanians, Assyrians, Chaldeans, Bactrians, Sacae, Scythians, Indians, Arians, Parthians, Chorasmians, Sogdians, Gandarians, Dadicae, Caspians, Sarangians, Pactyans, Utians, Myci, Paricanians, Arabians, Ethiopians, Libyans, Egyptians, Paphlagonians, Ligyans, Matieni, Mariandynians, Syrians (or Cappadocians), Phrygians, Armenians, Lydians, Mysians (or

[7]Herodotus, *op. cit.* VII 60–87.
[8]Herodotus, *op. cit.* VII 21.
[9]Herodotus, *op. cit.* VII 35.

Olympieni), Thracians, Pisidians, Cabalians, Milyans, Moschians, Tibareni, Macrones, Mossynoeci, Marians, Colchians, Alarodians and Saspires.[10] I have religiously copied Herodotus' list in order to underline the extent of the danger threatening the West in 480 BC. Three battles were fought, three of the most important battles in history: Thermopylae, Salamis and Plataea. At Thermopylae 4,000 Greeks, including 300 Spartans commanded by Leonidas, defended the pass leading into Greece against the Persian armies. When someone told Dioneces, one of the Spartan commanders, that the barbarians were so numerous that when they fired their arrows they hid the sun, he replied: 'So much the better, we shall be fighting in the shade.'[11] They were all killed bar one, and he was so ashamed of surviving that he committed suicide. Athens was invaded and all but destroyed, her citizens seeking shelter aboard their ships.

Salamis was a naval encounter. The Greeks had only 380[12] ships to pit against the Persians' 1,000,[13] so the Athenians boxed clever and drew the barbarians into a narrow stretch of water between the island of Salamis and the mainland where the enemy fleet found itself unable to manoeuvre. Xerxes, regarding the battle as his own private spectacle, installed himself and his entire entourage on the top of a hill. 'He had had a golden throne erected there and surrounded himself with a dense crowd of secretaries whose duty was to record the various stages of the battle.'[14] The Persians suffered a calamitous defeat.

The third battle was that of Plataea (479). Here, one year after the Persian invasion, the Greeks and their allies, commanded by the Spartan, Pausanias, finally put paid to the picturesque, if vast, army of barbarians. From this moment, Athens and Sparta were considered

---

[10]In Book VII of *The Histories* (61–79) Herodotus lists all the nationalities that took part in Xerxes' expedition, describing in detail the way they were dressed and the weapons they carried.

[11]Herodotus, *op. cit.* VII 226.

[12]According to Plutarch (*Themistocles* 14) they had 180.

[13]This number is confirmed by Aeschylus in *The Persians* (vv. 341–43):

Xerxes, as I know, commanded a fleet/ of one thousand ships, of which/ two hundred and seven/ were exceedingly swift. This/ is the precise number.

[14]Plutarch, *Themistocles* 13.

the greatest military powers of their time. The final honours of this championship struggle would be settled fifty years later during the Peloponnesian War.

Conflicts, with their dramatic immediacy, can often cause the people involved to mature at a greatly increased speed, and the Graeco-Persian Wars were no exception. In the years which followed the battle of Plataea, the city of Athens experienced a period so prosperous and intellectually fertile that it went down in history as the 'Golden Age of Pericles'. The seed-bed for this flowering was prepared by Themistocles and his *idée fixe* of the Hellenic League. More than 400 Greek cities decided to unite under the leadership of Athens and founded a kind of UNO with its headquarters on the island of Delos. Each *polis*, although retaining its independence, was obliged to subscribe a portion of its wealth in return for protection.

Pericles later decided that it would be safer for them all if the treasury was transferred to Athens, and from then on it was he who decided how the funds of the League should be utilized. This brilliant statesman thus secured the means for strengthening the Athenian fleet and, at the same time, for making good the damage caused by the Persians to the public buildings in Athens. Sparta predictably opted out of the pact. In the first place, she felt militarily self-sufficient, in the second, like all nations with a harsh regime (compare the Soviet Union today), she dared not open the door to such democratic and innovatory ideas as those proliferating in nearby Athens.

Greece has always been criticized for failing to become a single, strong, invincible nation during this period. Whether the rivalry between Athens and Sparta was to blame, or the lack of true Hellenic spirit in 'treacherous Thebes', the Greeks never managed to set up the unified state which, to many historians, seems to be a *sine qua non*. But instead, by remaining split up into a multitude of *poleis*, each with its individual character, she gave much more to humanity than yet another imperial power would have been capable of doing. A reflection of Grytzko Mascioni seems apt in this context: '. . . I am inclined – rashly – to the belief that the Greeks, with their *poleis*, designed once and for all the only social environment suitable for human habitation. No community can call itself truly civilized once it has grown too big for a real, even though theoretical, possibility for everyone to know or to come face to face with everyone else at some time or another. This, in the *polis*, was the case.'[15]

Pericles was an aristocrat, the son of a naval commander. In spite of this he rose to power by siding from the outset with the democratic party. It was a moment when anybody who had fought at Salamis or Plataea enjoyed a social standing equivalent to that of a hero of the Resistance, and as ex-combatants made up the majority of the *demos* (the voting public), the democratic process was bound to give him the victory.

Although a handsome man, Pericles had a strangely elongated cranium. This slight deformity earned him the nickname of *Schinocephalus*, or 'squill-head' (the squill is also known as the sea-onion).[16] Because of this the artists always represented him wearing a helmet and his biographers suggested that the protuberance was due to an overabundance of brain.

His teacher and spiritual mentor was Anaxagoras, and from him he learned 'the so-called higher philosophy, elevated speculation, a discourse that was lofty and free from plebeian and reckless effrontery, a composure of countenance that never relaxed into laughter, a grace of carriage and a way of draping his attire that suffered no disturbance from his movements while speaking, a modulation of voice that was never raised, and many similar characteristics which struck all his hearers with wondering amazement'.[17] He once listened imperturbably to a man who heaped abuse upon him for a whole day, and when evening came and he had to return home, he allowed the fellow to accompany him and thus continue his diatribe, and then ordered a servant to take a torch and escort the man safely to his own home.

Pericles was a great orator; his manner was calm and measured in political debate, but when his contemporaries refer to his haranguing the masses they use such terms as 'thundering', 'lightning' and 'wielding a dread thunderbolt in his tongue'.[18] Thanks to Zeno, from whom he learned rhetoric, he was also a formidable dialectician.

[15]Grytzko Mascioni, *Lo specchio greco,* Turin 1980, p. 245.
[16]Plutarch, *Life of Pericles* III.
[17]Plutarch, *Life of Pericles* V.
[18]Plutarch, *Life of Pericles* VIII.

When Archidamus, king of Sparta, asked Thucydides which was the abler wrestler out of himself and Pericles, Thucydides replied: 'Whenever I manage to throw him in wrestling, he disputes the fall and claims the point, and he even convinces those who saw him fall.'[19]

Pericles' ability in managing the affairs of the state is, however, beyond dispute. He realized, for example, the fundamental necessity of rewarding those who worked for the common good, and introduced pay for soldiers, administrators and even for magistrates. He also increased the number of public spectacles by organizing open-air banquets, processions and song festivals. In other words, he indulged the people's need for light entertainment. Among other things, he enabled the very poorest to attend by paying the admission charge for them out of state funds. In the field of the arts, he initiated one of the most creative periods in the history of man. Using the funds of the Delian League and taxes contributed by the richest citizens, he built dozens of sacred edifices and attracted the best artists of the age to Athens. For forty years Athens was transformed into a single, vast builder's yard. Every architect and every sculptor became a contractor in his own right, leading, as in the Renaissance workshops, a team of students and assistants. They used all manner of materials: marble, bronze, ivory, gold, ebony and cypress. When Pericles was eventually taken to task by some of the nobles for playing fast and loose with the public purse, he replied: 'Very well, then, from now on I shall build at my own expense. Of course, you understand that every edifice will bear the inscription of my name on its façade.'[20] His funds were immediately restored and he was given *carte blanche* to continue the work.

Pericles is also responsible for a change of attitude towards artists. Strange as it may seem, the ancient Greeks had little respect for those who dedicated their lives to producing works of sculpture and painting; this was due to their scornful attitude towards anyone who worked with his hands. The *banausi*, manual workers, were nearly always slaves or metics (resident aliens); the Hellenic ideal of life

---

[19]Plutarch, *Life of Pericles* VIII.
[20]Plutarch, *Life of Pericles* XIV.

excluded any lucrative activity and aimed, instead, at the greatest possible amount of leisure.[21] *A propos* of this attitude, I had an uncle who used to declare proudly, 'Although I say it myself, I have never done a day's work!' and he said it, I assure you, without irony. According to Aristotle, the performance of menial tasks was degrading and should be left to menials, while education and nobility of soul were the exclusive preserve of the master class.[22] And Plutarch tells us that in Greece no well-bred young man, however much he might have admired the Zeus at Pisa (Olympia) or the Hera at Argos, would, for that reason, ever have wished to be Phidias or Polycleitus, for 'it does not of necessity follow that, if the work delights you with its grace, the one who wrought it is worthy of your esteem'.[23] When Philip of Macedonia heard his son playing the lute exceptionally well, he is said to have reprimanded him by asking the boy: 'Are you not ashamed of yourself for playing so well?' In other words, Philip was scandalized at the thought of the hours of study and practice evidenced by such mastery of the instrument.

Pericles' attitude was quite the opposite of this: he loved to surround himself with great masters and, in particular, nominated Phidias as his adviser where the plastic arts were concerned. Scandalmongers hinted that Phidias not only supplied him with statues but with models too. The sculptor was in fact accused of setting up assignations in his own studio between the statesman and certain ladies of good social standing. Pericles, let's make no bones about it, was something of a ladies' man. When he was in the army he apparently even seduced the wife of his immediate commander, the redoubtable Menippus, and he was later charged publicly by Stesimbrotus for consorting with his own daughter-in-law.[24]

His one true love, however, was the celebrated Aspasia, the beautiful Ionian woman whose relationship with Pericles caused him to be charged with concubinage. Aspasia was born in Miletus, where, according to malicious gossip, she had once worked as a prostitute. On her arrival in Athens she was introduced to Pericles by a col-

[21]See H. D. F. Kitto, *The Greeks*, p. 134.
[22]Aristotle, *Politics* III 1277a.
[23]Plutarch, *Life of Pericles* II.
[24]Plutarch, *Life of Pericles* XIII.

league, Thargelia, whose advice was: 'If you've got to sell yourself, choose men of power.'[25]

Once settled in Athens, Aspasia indulged in an enterprise somewhere between a radical-chic *salon* and a brothel, where the most intelligent men could meet the most beautiful women and exchange ideas. There is a story that one day, following a fatal accident in a javelin contest, Pericles and Protagoras spent an entire afternoon there discussing whether the javelin-thrower, the judges, the dead man or the javelin was to blame for the accident. Even Socrates and his pupils were known to be frequent visitors to the *salon*, though whether the discussion group or the girls furnished the chief inducement is unknown.

Aspasia was the perfect hostess, gracious, cultured and of refined taste. It was rumoured that more than one of Pericles' initiatives had its origin with her rather than with him, for instance the decision to intervene on the side of Miletus during the quarrel with Samos. We should not allow ourselves to be prejudiced by her apparently shady profession. The upper-class ladies of her day were nearly always ignorant, whereas the prostitutes received an excellent education. Bear in mind that the word 'prostitute', *pornai* or *pallacai* in Greek, was a label attached to her by the enemies of Pericles, while the historians never refer to her as anything other than a hetaera. Imagine us, today, referring to the Japanese geishas as whores!

Aspasia also bore Pericles a son, though he was never able to claim citizenship as this required that both parents should be Athenian.

The laws of the democracy gave plenty of scope to Pericles' adversaries and many of his friends suffered in consequence. Anaxagoras was hauled before the judges and only saved his life by fleeing the city; Phidias was accused of embezzling the gold supplied for his work, and although he proved himself innocent by removing the gold from the statue in question and having it weighed, he was thrown into prison where he died, so it was rumoured, of poison; Aspasia was charged with impiety by the comic poet Hermippus, and also accused by him of aiding and abetting prostitution; she only escaped

[25]Plutarch, *Life of Pericles* XXIV.

imprisonment thanks to Pericles 'shedding copious tears and entreating the jurors'.[26]

Meanwhile, even greater troubles were brewing outside. Sparta, alarmed by the fact that right next door life was being treated as if it were an enjoyable adventure, was itching to pick a fight with Athens. For several years Pericles avoided war (some say he was giving bribes to the Spartan generals), but the time came when there was nothing more he could do, and the conflict exploded in all its fury. The prudent Pericles, whom Plutarch, in his *Parallel Lives*, coupled astutely with Fabius Maximus, refused to be drawn into battle and chose to barricade himself and his army in Athens and await the attack. Unfortunately for him, the influx of thousands upon thousands of country-dwellers, who had been forced to abandon their homes and take refuge within the walls, caused a terrible pestilence to break out in the city and Pericles was held chiefly responsible. He was stripped of his command and sentenced to pay a fine of fifteen talents.[27]

In the autumn of 429 Pericles himself became a victim of the pestilence. On the day of his death all his friends gathered around his bed, and thinking that he had slipped into a coma, began to recall his achievements on behalf of the city over the past forty years. But Pericles was not unconscious, and eventually spoke out: 'Many of these things were due to fortune,' he said, 'and you have forgotten to mention my fairest title to your admiration, which is that no living Athenian ever put on mourning because of me'.[28]

[26]Plutarch, *Life of Pericles* XXXII.
[27]Plutarch, *Life of Pericles* XXXV.
[28]Plutarch, *Life of Pericles* XXXVIII.

XIX
Anaxagoras

rank Sinatra is called *The Voice*; Anaxagoras was nick-named *Nous*, the Mind. In each case, the identification of the personality with his predominant characteristic seems to have hit the nail on the head. No one better than Anaxagoras, certainly, could have been chosen to typify the intellectual ferment of fifth-century Athens. The contemporary love of dialectic, interest in natural phenomena, the new medicine of Hippocrates, the purity of architectonic line and even the geometrical simplicity of the layout of the Piraeus (planned by Hippodamus of Miletus) all bear witness to the determination of thinkers and practical men alike to interpret their world by mental resources alone. The gods were out of fashion as far as the intelligentsia was concerned, and soon became, for this very reason, useful tools in the hands of the reactionaries for beating their opponents over the head. Aristotle said: 'When Anaxagoras affirmed that Mind is present in nature, he appeared like a sober man among a crowd of drunkards compared with the futile theorists who preceded him.'[1]

Anaxagoras, son of Hegesibulus,[2] was born between 500 and 497 BC in Clazomenae, a small Ionian town close to Smyrna. He was a pupil of Diogenes of Apollonia, Anaximenes' successor, and, like all the philosophers who came under the influence of the Milesian school, spent more time gazing at the heavens than looking after his

[1] Aristotle, *Metaphysics* A 3 984b 15.
[2] Diogenes Laertius, *op. cit.* II 6.

own interests. This exasperated his family, but when they exclaimed: 'For goodness' sake, why don't you look after your property?' he retorted, 'Why don't you look after it instead?'[3] And to avoid further bother he distributed all he had among his relatives. The young Anaxagoras, in fact, was never really happy unless he was on his own at the top of Mount Mimas gazing at the stars.[4] He would camp there throughout the night, wrapped in a woollen blanket and total silence. Once, when a neighbour reproved him with indifference to his native land, he replied: 'You are quite mistaken: I am greatly concerned with my native land,' and pointed to the sky.

His astronomical observations soon made him famous. People said that he had learnt the secrets of the universe directly from the 'occult books' of the Egyptian priests and credited him with all kinds of predictions such as a solar eclipse, an earthquake (he had observed mud moving in the bottom of a well),[5] the collapse of a building and even the fall of a meteorite into the Aegispotamus.[6] Divination fascinated the Greeks: anyone who was able to predict a natural phenomenon, whether by calculation or sheer good luck, was made for life. Anaxagoras, for instance, was always introduced as 'the man who predicted the stone falling from the sky'. Another happy forecast occurred at the Olympics: he appeared with his head covered by a sheepskin as if to keep it dry, and although the sky had been quite clear up to then, sure enough it soon started to pour with rain.[7]

When he was twenty he went to Athens and there founded a school of philosophy. Among his students were Euripides and Archelaus; the latter became famous as the teacher (and possibly the lover) of Socrates and 'for explaining the production of sound as being the concussion of the air'.[8]

According to some historians, Anaxagoras was summoned to Athens by Pericles' father, Xanthippus, to act as tutor to his son; according to others, however, he came to Greece as a Persian soldier

[3]Diogenes Laertius, *op. cit.* II 7.
[4]Philostratus, *Life of Apollonius of Tyana* II 5.
[5]Ammanius Marcellinus, *Histories* XXII 16, 22.
[6]Pliny, *Natural History* II 149–50.
[7]Diogenes Laertius, *op. cit.* II 8 [changed]
[8]Diogenes Laertius, *op. cit.* II 17.

in Xerxes' army, which would explain the charge of 'Medism' levelled at him thirty years later by Pericles' enemies.[9] According to one version of the story of his trial, he was accused by Thucydides[10] of treasonable correspondence with the Persians and 'impiety', or bringing religion into disrepute. It is said that the sentence was passed by a very small majority.[11] Despite being the highest authority in Athens, there was nothing Pericles could do except bribe the gaolers to let Anaxagoras escape before sentence was pronounced. The truth was that poor Anaxagoras' only crime was his friendship with Pericles. When it came to damaging a political rival, the Greeks were not oversubtle: a word of criticism against Zeus was quite sufficient grounds for an accusation.

Anaxagoras' exile was hard, if for no other reason than that it banished him from the 'cultural centre', but he was too proud and, above all, too wise to complain. On being informed of the death sentence his only comment was: 'Long ago nature condemned both my judges and myself to death',[12] and when told that his sons were dead, he said simply: 'I knew that my children were born to die.' To one who enquired if he missed the society of the Athenians, he replied, 'No, but they miss mine,'[13] and to another, who sympathized with him because he was dying in a foreign land, he said, 'From whatever place we start, the descent to Hades is much the same.'

Meantime, his book was circulating clandestinely among the intellectuals. According to Plutarch, 'It was still under seal of secrecy, and made its way slowly among a few only, who received it with a certain caution . . .'[14] The book was without doubt the first best seller, and has the distinction of being the first whose price we know for sure: it cost one drachma.[15]

As we hinted before, there are several mutually contradictory

[9]Diogenes Laertius, *op. cit.* II 11.
[10]Thucydides, son of Melisias, leader of the aristocratic faction. Not to be confused with the historian Thucydides.
[11]Josephus, *Against Apion* II 265.
[12]Diogenes Laertius, *op. cit.* II 13.
[13]Diogenes Laertius, *op. cit.* II 10.
[14]Plutarch, *Life of Nicias* 23.
[15]Plato, *Apology* 26.

versions of Anaxagoras' trial. Some sources give the date as 450, others as 432, some say that he was impeached by Thucydides, others Cleon,[16] and the sentence is variously described as capital punishment, ostracism or a fine of five talents. The most likely solution is that there were two trials and two sentences passed with an interval of eighteen years between them.[17]

Ostracism[18] was a kind of negative election that took place once a year in early winter. Provided there was a consensus of 6,000 Athenians, any citizen could be removed from the scene for five or ten years without even knowing why. Given that the vote was by means of a secret ballot and that one might be perfectly innocent, you can imagine how easy it was to find oneself banished. In actual fact none of the great Athenians of the fifth century – apart from Pericles – escaped impeachment. Even Aristides 'the just' suffered a period of exile. Ostracism was intended to affirm the supremacy of the *demos* over the individual, to apply a brake to the cult of personality; in practice it turned out to be a powerful tool in the hands of a few jealous people.

The second trial, assuming it took place, opened with the flogging of a slave who confessed to having heard Anaxagoras speak of the sun as a red-hot stone carried round by the rotation of the ether.[19] The crime was a serious one. A few years earlier a certain Diopeithes had managed to get a law passed which made it a criminal offence to deny the existence of the gods or to teach any doctrines regarding the heavens.[20] Pericles rushed to his friend's defence and did everything he could to get him acquitted. He brought him to court still feverish from a recent illness and, pointing to the haggard face of his old teacher, asked: 'Athenians, have you any fault to find with the way in which I have always endeavoured to serve the interests of the city? Well, I am the pupil of this man!'[21] The judges released Anaxagoras – more out of pity for his infirmities than because they were swayed by

[16]Plutarch, *Life of Pericles* XXXII.
[17]Cf. *I Presocratici*, cit., vol. II, p. 563, n. 19.
[18]J. Burckhardt, *op. cit.* [ref. to follow].
[19]Diogenes Laertius, *op. cit.* II, 12. (See also Plato, *Apology* 26 D.)
[20]Plutarch, *Life of Pericles* XXXII.
[21]Diogenes Laertius, *op. cit.* II 13.

Pericles' impassioned defence – but the humiliation was too great for the unfortunate philosopher and he starved himself to death in Lampsacus, a tiny village in the north of Ionia. Lying on his bed with his face already muffled in a grave-cloth, he complained to Pericles, who had come to visit him, that he had never been paid for his teaching, and 'even those who need a lamp pour oil therein'.[22] Just before his death the archons of Lampsacus enquired how he would like to be commemorated, and he asked for the children to be given a holiday.[23]

With all respect to 'Mister Mind', I admit to finding the character of Anaxagoras unsympathetic. In particular, I am put off by the report that no one ever saw him smile. Had this been due to some character defect one could forgive him, but it was not; the dour solemnity of expression was part of a deliberate pattern of behaviour. And it was in deference to him that his favourite disciples, Euripides[24] and Pericles,[25] refused to drink in company or take part in symposia for fear of being surprised with a smile on their lips. Come to think of it, this aversion to smiling is very widespread even in our own day, particularly among Italian intellectuals. Try watching how they behave in television interviews and you cannot fail to be struck by the expression of lofty austerity. Heaven knows what obscure Calvinistic influences made up of guilt complexes and desire for expiation make them so allergic to any hint of fun. Maybe the Latin motto *risus abundat in ore stultorum* was actually put about by some ancestor of Moravia, Sciascia or Giorgio Bocca. Luckily, every now and then an Einstein or a Bertrand Russell appears and the cultural climate brightens perceptibly.

The questions asked by Anaxagoras are the classical questions of pre-Socratic philosophy:

1 What are the primordial elements?
2 Who or what animates them?

[22]Plutarch, *Life of Pericles* XVI.
[23]Diogenes Laertius, *op. cit.* II 14.
[24]Aulus Gellius, *Noctes Atticae*, XV 20.
[25]Plutarch, *Life of Pericles* VII.

For Anaxagoras the primal substances were infinite both in number and quality; he called them *homoeomeries*. So we are not dealing with a single *archè*, as did the Milesian school, nor with four different elements, as did Empedocles, but with an infinite number of infinitesimal particles, logically arranged in an order established by Mind (*Nous*).

To begin with, says Anaxagoras, these *homoeomeries* were all jumbled together as if in a giant food-mixer with no discernible differentiation of colour or any other characteristic[26] – until Mind suddenly intervened and the 'food-mixer' began to spin round, separating out the contents by centrifugal force. Then 'the dense and the cold and the moist and the dark came together where the earth is now, while the rare and the warm and the dry (and the bright) went outwards towards the further part of the ether' (R.P. 156).

While the *homoeomeries* are described as infinitesimal particles of matter, homogeneous, and invisible on account of their exiguity, every object that we see, no matter how minute, contains all the possible *homoeomeries*. In other words, 'everything has a portion of everything hidden within it, but only that which is most numerous will be apparent'.[27] That means that in a wooden table there is something of everything, even fire, smoke, ash and so on, but the reason that it appears to us only as wood is because the *homoeomeries* of wood are present in greater quantities than any other kind.

In support of his theory Anaxagoras reminds us that the food eaten by animals is transformed into flesh, bones, hairs, veins, gristle, nails and even horns, and since hair cannot be made of what is not hair, it follows that there must be *homoeomeries* of hair present in the food itself.[28]

Having reasoned that 'everything is in everything', the philosopher goes on to say that everything contains not only its most characteristic properties but also their opposites: snow, for instance, appears white but must also contain a portion of black.[29] This reminds me of my

[26]fr. 4 Diels-Kranz.
[27]Lucretius, *De rerum natura* I 810ff.
[28]Aetios, *op. cit.* i. 3, 5.
[29]Sextus Empiricus, *Pyrrhonian Hypotyposes* i. 33.

mother saying, when she found the soup insipid, *è dolce 'e sale*, meaning 'it's been salted with sugar'.

Anaxagoras argued against the theories of Empedocles: like, he said, does not seek out like but its opposite. Opposite qualities owe their very existence to the enemy. Each of us feels the sensation of cold, for example, in proportion to the heat of our own body, and a sound which may be almost inaudible amid the bustle of the *agora*, can be heard in the still of the night.

We can only understand Anaxagoras' system properly if we have a clear idea of what he meant by Mind. As we have already explained, his *Nous* has nothing to do with God, not being a creative principle but only a 'material' substance albeit possessing qualities such as purity and rarefaction in a super-refined form. *Nous* is only present in living things and is responsible for the ordering of the universe as we perceive it and not for the creation of primordial substances. It is called Mind because, unlike Chance, it is aware of what it does.

The limited responsibility of *Nous* in Anaxagoras' system was something of a disappointment to the Athenian philosophers, so much so that we find Plato, in the *Phaedo*, putting these words into the mouth of Socrates:[30]

I once heard someone reading from a book by Anaxagoras, and asserting that it is Mind that produces order and is the cause of everything. This explanation pleased me. Somehow it seemed right that Mind should be the cause of everything; and I reflected that if this is so, Mind in producing order sets everything in order and arranges each individual thing in the way that is best for it ... These reflections made me suppose, to my delight, that in Anaxagoras I had found an authority on causation after my own heart. I assumed that he would begin by informing us whether the earth is flat or round, and would then proceed to explain in detail the reason and logical necessity for this ... It was a wonderful hope, my friend, but it was quickly dashed. As I read on I discovered that the fellow made no use of Mind and assigned to it no causality for the order of the world, but adduced causes like air and ether and water and many other absurdities.

[30]Plato, *Phaedo*, 97 B. (Trans. by Hugh Tredennick).

Besides *Nous*, Anaxagoras was also called *ho physikótatos*, 'the great physicist', on account of his passion for natural science. Here for you to sample are a few of his basic ideas about physics and astronomy:

- The stars are fiery stones that rotate at tremendous speed in the sky until a sudden slowing down causes them to fall to earth (this theory may have had its origin in the fall of the meteorite at Aegispotamo).[31]
- 'The Sun sends light to the Moon'[32] which is a cold stone.
- The orbit of the Moon, being lower than that of the Sun, determines eclipses.[33]
- A lion called Nemeus fell out of the Moon.[34]
- The Moon is inhabited, and moreover has hills, ravines and houses upon it just like ours.[35]
- The winds are produced by rarefaction of the air warmed by the Sun.[36]
- Thunder occurs when the clouds collide.
- Earthquakes are caused by the movement of masses of air imprisoned in the depths of the Earth.
- Comets are formed by a conjunction of planets which emit flames, and shooting stars are sparks thrown off by the air.[37]
- The Sun is bigger than the Peloponnese.[38]

As you can see, Anaxagoras was a trier: in some cases he hit the nail on the head, in others he missed by a mile. But we must try to put ourselves into the shoes of these ancient scientists who had to feel their way largely by guesswork, trusting in part to the evidence of the naked eye and in part to fantasy.

Anaxagoras too had his own evolutionary theory. The first men originated from water and were later born from each other, the males from the right side of the womb, the females from the left.[39] Men soon became the most intelligent beings in the universe because they

[31]Hippolytus, *Refutation of all Heresies* I 8, 6.
[32]Plutarch, *On the Face of the Moon's Disk* 16; 929 B.
[33]Hippolytus, *op. cit.* I 8, 9.
[34]Cf. *I Presocratici, cit.*, vol. II, p. 585.
[35]Diogenes Laertius, *op. cit.* II 8.
[36]Hippolytus, *op. cit.* I 8, 11ff.
[37]Diogenes Laertius, *op. cit.* II 9.
[38]Diogenes Laertius, *op. cit.* II 8.
[39]Hippolytus, *op. cit.* I 8, 12.

had hands. This was a stroke of genius and one that modern experts, ethologists and palaeontologists in particular, tend to agree with, but it was severely criticized in his own day. Aristotle, for example, took issue with him over it: 'According to Anaxagoras, man is the wisest of beings because he has hands. In my view it would have been more reasonable to say he has hands because he is the wisest.'[40]

---

[40]Aristotle, *De partibus animalium* IV 10 687a 7.

XX

Leucippus

A couple of words about Leucippus, for the very good reason that to find any more to say about him would be hard. Of his date of birth we know precious little: historians have cautiously placed it between 490 and 470 BC. About his town of origin their opinions differ:[1] some say Miletus, some Elea, some Abdera and some nowhere at all. The last of these theories finds a champion in Epicurus,[2] no less, who, although professing admiration for the Atomists, denies that there was ever a philosopher called Leucippus. To us, quite honestly, Epicurus seems to be somewhat chancing his arm here: in his book *On Coming to Be and Passing Away*, Aristotle mentions Leucippus' name eleven times, and it is decidedly unlikely that anyone as punctilious as Aristotle should have held forth at length about an imaginary philosopher. Lastly, there is also Tannery's theory, according to which Leucippus was merely a pseudonym of Democritus.

Be that as it may, for the purposes of this thumbnail sketch of Leucippus I am quite prepared to believe that he was born in 480, give or take a decade, and that he stayed in his native town until the revolt of the aristocrats in 450. Once turned thirty, he set off on his travels like all the respectable pre-Socratics, and travelled extensively. We hear reports of his having been to Elea, where he remained long enough to learn and demolish the doctrine of Zeno, and Abdera, a

[1]Diogenes Laertius, *op. cit.* IX 30ff.
[2]Diogenes Laertius, *op. cit.* X 13.

Thracian city half-way between Greece and Ionia, where he founded a school of philosophy.

The insubstantial Leucippus was unlucky enough to have as his pupil the celebrated Democritus, and it was the fame of the pupil that eclipsed that of the master so completely that doubts were raised about the very existence of the latter. To begin with, Democritus never so much as deigned to mention his teacher in any of his numerous books, and historians, with the odd exception,[3] invariably quote the two together, making it difficult to distinguish the thought of one from that of the other. One of Leucippus' treatises, *The Great Diacosmos*, was included in the *Corpus Democriteum* and ended up as just another work by Democritus.

Having admitted the difficulties, we shall nevertheless attempt, within the limits of this modest survey of philosophers, to reappraise Leucippus, crediting him with the invention of two concepts fundamental to the history of ideas: the void and the atom.

Until this moment everyone had striven to deny the existence of the void. Empedocles, with the experiment of the girl dipping her brass vessel (*klepsydra*) into the water, had demonstrated that what the common man referred to as 'air' had substance and in no way corresponded to the void. Anaxagoras also found a practical way of demonstrating the 'substantiality' of air by means of an inflated wineskin. And lastly, Parmenides had not only denied the existence of the void but had used this argument to prove that there was no such thing as movement: 'The One', he had said, 'is fixed within itself, having no space in which to change or move.'[4]

Regarding atoms, we must not forget that Anaxagoras had got very close with his *homoeomeries*. It is most unlikely, however, that the two philosophers, being contemporaries and living in different places, should have influenced each other, and there is, in any case, a substantial difference between the *homoeomeries* of Anaxagoras and the atoms of Leucippus: the first were infinitely divisible, the second, though minute, were conceived as solid particles incapable of being

---

[3]Diogenes Laertius, *op. cit.* IX 30 *n.* and 46 (where Theophrastus is also quoted as attributing a work to Leucippus).
[4]Plato, *Theaetetus* 180 e.

split and therefore, practically speaking, as the smallest parts into which matter could be divided. 'Atom' is the Greek word for 'indivisible'.

XXI
Democritus

Democritus, the son of Hegesistratus or Atheno-critus or Damasippus, was born in either Abdera or Miletus[1] at a date which varies between 472 and 457 BC. The register of pre-Socratic births is its usual vague self, a list of haphazard dates and putative paternity. But put yourself in the shoes of these ancient Greeks: they had no real calendar so if they were asked to supply the year of their birth all they could do was refer to the archons in power at the time or to Olympic victors. It's like my telling you that I was born in the year that Jesse Owens won the hundred metres, and married when Tambroni was President of the Council of Ministers. Now you know – or do you?!

Democritus was the youngest of four. He had two brothers, Herodotus and Damastes, and a sister whose name is unknown. The family was wealthy and he lacked for nothing as a boy; then, when his father died, he renounced his share of the land and took a certain sum of money instead. It must have been a considerable sum: Diogenes mentions 'over a hundred talents', which was a fortune.[2] Democritus accepted the money against his own moral convictions only because it was necessary to further a project he had been dreaming about for years: to travel the world and meet as many teachers as possible. Horace, the great Latin poet, comments on his action as follows: 'No

[1]Diogenes Laertius, *op. cit.* IX 34.
[2]Diogenes Laertius, *op. cit.* IX 36.

marvel if the beasts enter Democritus' fields and consume the harvest, when his spirit, forgetful of his body, rushes swiftly hither and thither.'[3]

Democritus was a tireless traveller. He studied astronomy with the Chaldeans, theology with the Magi, geometry with the Egyptians; he visited Ethiopia, the Red Sea and even India, where he encountered the Gymnosophists.[4] In a fragment quoted by Clement of Alexandria[5] he says: 'I am, among my contemporaries, the one who has travelled over the greater part of the earth, seeking out of all things the most curious; I saw lands without number and listened to most of the learned men; and in the composition of geometrical figures, with their relative demonstrations, no one was superior to me, not even the so-called *arpedonapti*.' On these travels he had constant help from the Persian royal family, and the reason for this, according to one story, was that his father had entertained Xerxes when he was crossing Thrace during the second Graeco–Persian war, and the family had enjoyed a measure of protection from the Persian king ever afterwards.[6]

Obviously such an extensive tour could not fail to take in Athens, and here, strange though it may seem, 'no one recognized him'.[7] There are those who suggest that the unnamed young man who converses with Socrates in Plato's *The Rivals*[8] may have been Democritus.[9] This is indeed the dialogue in which Socrates compares the philosopher to a pentathlete, a man capable of coming first in the final classification without having won in any single discipline, and Democritus boasted of being an expert in Physics, Ethics, Encyclopaedic Sciences, the Arts and Mathematics.

When he finally went home after all this travelling he was without a drachma to his name; all he could do was go and live with his brothers as a poor relation. Then the government notified him that, in

---

[3]Horace, *Epistles* I 12, 12.
[4]Diogenes Laertius, *op. cit.* IX 35.
[5]Clement of Alexandria, *Miscellanies* I 15, 69.
[6]Diogenes Laertius, *op. cit.* IX 34.
[7]Cicero, *Tusculanae disputationes* V 36, 104.
[8]Plato, *The Rivals* 136a.
[9]Diogenes Laertius, *op. cit.* IX 37.

accordance with an ancient Thracian law, he would be denied burial in his homeland as one who had squandered his inheritance. So, not relishing the thought of being thrown into the sea, Democritus read his book *The Great Diacosmos* in public, and the Abderites were so dazzled by its brilliance that they not only guaranteed him a funeral at state expense but refunded his hundred talents.[10]

Odd fish, Democritus: to some he was a *bon viveur*, always ready for a laugh or a joke, to others he was a scholarly recluse. He was probably both: there must have been a reason for his having two nicknames, 'The Laughing Philosopher' and 'Wisdom'.[11] His roars of laughter were so famous in Greece that he was criticized several times by Athenian intellectuals. It was said of him: 'He comes from Abdera, the town of idiots.'[12] The chief butt of Democritus' satire was Anaxagoras. The Abderite philosopher was always twitting him for his theory of the Intellect and he also accused him of plagiarizing certain ancient doctrines regarding the Sun and the Moon.[13] The basic reason for all this animosity, however, appears to be that Anaxagoras had turned him down when he applied for admission to the school of Athens.[14]

A tendency to introversion was apparent from Democritus' boyhood. As a child he had built himself a hut at the bottom of the garden, a kind of den where he could hide away from everyone. And as a man, we hear, he spent long periods in desert solitudes or among the tombs in cemeteries in order to exercise his imagination to the full.[15]

His experiences in the Orient had given him certain divinatory powers: apart from predicting natural phenomena (the occupation to which all philosophers were by now dedicating themselves), Democritus frequently dazzled his friends by some really amazing feat. We read of him once drinking a cup of milk and saying: 'This has been milked from a black she-goat which has produced her first

[10]Diogenes Laertius, *op. cit.* IX 39–40.
[11]See *I Presocratici, cit.*, Vol. II, p. 668.
[12]See *I Presocratici, cit.*, Vol. II, p. 697.
[13]Diogenes Laertius, *op, cit.* IX 34.
[14]Diogenes Laertius, *op. cit.* IX 35.
[15]Diogenes Laertius, *op. cit.* IX 38.

kid,'[16] and the statement was immediately verified. Another time, he greeted a serving-girl accompanying Hippocrates with the words: 'Good morning, maiden,' but when he met her the next day he greeted her with: 'Good morning, woman'; the girl had, in fact, had her first sexual encounter during the intervening night. The historians say nothing about the name of her partner, but were Hippocrates to have been involved, Democritus' intuition may have had more to do with the confidential communication of a friend than with a phenomenon of parapsychology.

One day, not knowing how to console Darius the Great for the loss of his wife, Democritus said to him: 'Procure for me everything I have listed here and I promise to bring her back to life''. The king immediately set to and tried to fulfill the sage's every wish, but the last item defeated him, that of inscribing on the queen's tomb the names of three men who had never suffered grief. At which Democritus said: 'O unreasonable man, you weep unrestrainedly as if you were the only man who ever experienced such a calamity!'[17]

Legend has it that when he was a very old man, Democritus deliberately blinded himself by gazing at the rays of the sun reflected in a silvered shield, not wanting 'the bodily vision to impede the vision of the soul'.[18] According to Tertullian, however, the aged voluptuary was more concerned with avoiding the sight of beautiful women now that he could no longer make love to them.[19] Whatever the motive, we have an independent source for this dramatic incident in a poem by Laberius Decimus:[20]

> *Democritus of Abdera, philosopher of nature,*
> *turned a shield directly towards that quarter of the*
> *   heavens in which Hyperion rises*
> *to blind himself with celestial splendour,*
> *and thus with the rays of the sun destroyed*
> *   the light of his eyes.*

[16]Diogenes Laertius, *op. cit.* IX 42.
[17]Julian the Apostate, *Letters*, no. 201.
[18]Cicero, *Tusculanae disputationes* V 39, 114.
[19]Tertullian, *Apologeticum* 46.
[20]Aulus Gellius, *Noctes Atticae* X 17.

In one of his books he had once written: 'Longevity is often not a long life but a long death.'[21] In fact, when he was over a hundred he decided to commit suicide and took less and less nourishment each day until he was eating nothing at all; but when he was on the point of dying, his sister, also a centenarian, complained that his death would prevent her from attending the festival of Thesmophoria, so the philosopher patiently requested hot loaves to be brought to him and put under his nose. By just inhaling the scent he held on for another three days, then asked his sister if the festival were now over, and when she said 'yes', closed his eyes for ever.[22]

Diogenes Laertius dedicated the following lines to him:

> *For three days he entertained Death in his house*
> *on nothing but the warm smell of the loaves.*

His fame spread throughout the civilized world. Even Timon of Phlius spoke well of him.[23] Plato, however, was his most implacable enemy: he refused to mention him and even attempted to have his books burned. He was foiled in this by one factor: the writings of Democritus were diffused all over the world and had been received everywhere with enthusiasm.[24]

Democritus' doctrine is simplicity itself; not so, maybe, the questions he avoided, but we shall come to that in due time. First things first.

Reality is made up of atoms and the void.[25] The atoms are infinite in number, absolutely compact and therefore physically indivisible, qualitatively similar but differing in geometrical form and in size. The void, on the other hand, is simply empty space, a 'no-thing' (*oudén*) that must be allowed to exist on exactly the same terms as the 'something' (*dén*).[26] To explain it in even more elementary terms, the world is described as being made of minute particles of very hard

---

[21]Porphyry, *De abstinentia* IV 21.
[22]Diogenes Laertius, *op. cit.* IX 43.
[23]Diogenes Laertius, *op. cit.* IX 40.
[24]J. Bollack, 'Un silence de Platon', *Revue de philologie* 41, 1967, p. 242ff.
[25]Bertrand Russell, *op. cit.* p. 83.
[26]In Greek, *dén* signifies being, while *oudén*, not being, means 'nothing'.

matter in various forms, little balls, cubes, dodecahedrons and so on, which move around in a physical space made of nothing. These particles, called atoms, sometimes adhere to each other and sometimes separate off.[27]

If we accept this description of the world around us, some questions occur immediately: who made the atoms and the void, who causes the atoms to move, who gave them the first push, who sticks them together or pulls them apart? And Democritus is less convincing on this point; all he can say is that the atoms are infinite in number and have always existed,[28] and, similarly, have always moved in the void. Whirling around as if in a vortex (*dínos*), they collide with one another from time to time. The resulting rebounds (*apopàllesthai*), collisions (*palmós*), passing touches (*epíspasis*) and deflections (*sunkroúesthai*) cause the formation of clusters, and these are the objects we see around us. Democritus dismisses the theory of Empedocles, according to which union and separation are governed by Love and Strife; he takes his materialism more seriously and regards concepts such as Love and Strife as smacking too much of mythology: one might as well go back to Zeus and Saturn, who, if nothing else, were more amusing.

This, then, is the substance of Democritus' physical and cosmological theory. The flaw in it is, I think, self-evident. If we accept that the atoms have been eddying around 'for ever', we have to assume one of two hypotheses: either that they follow parallel courses, in which case one is left to wonder how the first collision ever took place (given that they couldn't change lanes there would have been an almighty pile-up!), or that the paths were not parallel and that collisions took place from the start. But what 'start' are we talking about, since we have only just said that the atoms have been in motion 'for ever'?

Epicurus, who admired Democritus and was a convinced Atomist, later tried to put his finger in the breach by suggesting[29] that the atoms differ from each other in size and weight, and that this diversity

[27]Cicero, *De finibus* I 6, 17.
[28]Plutarch, *Stromata* 7.
[29]Aetios i. 3, 18.

caused them to take a downward path.[30] With apologies to Epicurus, our objection stands.

In the world of the Atomists there is no place for anything which is not a *plenum* or a void; even spirit, thought and sensation are material substances, the atoms of the spirit being merely rounder, smoother and more mobile than those of the body. Life is sustained as long as a man, by breathing, succeeds in holding the atoms of the air and those of the spirit in equilibrium. Sensation is produced in the following way: every object emits an 'effluence', a physical if invisible substance called *éidolon* that collides with the intervening air and, after a series of chain reactions, eventually impinges upon the atoms of the senses, which, in their turn, transmit the impact to the atoms of thought.[31] Thus everything is accomplished by physical contacts. Knowledge is subjective in that it depends upon the intervening link and upon the capacity of the receptor. Had Polaroids been around in Democritus' day, he would have been able to show everybody what *éidola* were made of.

The main difference between Democritus' atoms and the *homoeomeries* of Anaxagoras lies in the divisibility of matter. Both theories specify minute particles, but while the atom is an exceedingly hard particle impervious to any attack from outside, the *homoeomeria* is at least theoretically capable of infinite division. Following the line of Anaxagoras' reasoning, every molecule of our body could contain millions and millions of worlds, inhabited or not, and this can never be disproved since we have no more access to the infinitesimal within us than we have to the galaxies in space.

The crux of the problem is the existence or non-existence of the void. Strange as it may seem, this problem has still not been resolved. We now accept that there is no empty space in nature; even where we get closest to this, we still have light-waves. Democritus said that we can only cut an apple because the blade of the knife finds spaces through which it can penetrate, but this line of reasoning is no longer tenable because, since Einstein, the distinction between matter and space has disappeared. This is a very difficult concept and I apologize

---

[30] *Parénklisis* in Epicurus' terminology, *clinamen* in Lucretius'.
[31] Aetios iv. 13, 1.

to the reader for introducing it, but relativity theory had the effect, as it were, of indissolubly marrying space and time. 'Not matter . . . but events are the *stuff* of the world, and each of them is of brief duration. In this respect, modern physics is on the side of Heraclitus as against Parmenides.'[32]

To a certain extent, Democritus was trying to reconcile the two currents of thought most characteristic of his century: the theories of Being and of Becoming. The supporters of Being held that the One was immovable, eternal and indivisible; the fans of Becoming argued that there was nothing in the world that was not in motion or that could be compared with itself even after a second. What could one do? To Democritus, the way to bring these two theories into alignment was to invent atomism. He agrees with Parmenides about the atom, specified as something immutable, eternal, indivisible and containing no empty space, thus conceding to the Eleatic all the prerogatives of the One except immobility. To Heraclitus he concedes the void, a physical space where atoms can move freely and where matter can congeal and separate out in a continual Becoming.

The philosophers who came after him were unhappy about this. Socrates, Plato and Aristotle were constantly hoping for someone to come along and shed light upon the first cause and the ultimate purpose. To them Democritus was like a dramatist who had skipped the first and last acts of a play. Nor would it have solved the problem had they rushed to his aid affirming that atoms had been set in motion by a Creator: Democritus, out-and-out materialist that he was, would have immediately asked, 'And who created the Creator?' The truth is that Philosophy, ever oscillating between Science and Religion, had touched an extremity with the Atomists, all Science and no Religion.

[32]Bertrand Russell, *op. cit.*, p. 87.

XXII
The Sophists

dvocacy, as a profession, was invented by the Greeks in the fifth century BC. Unlike the discovery of fire and penicillin, that of the advocate came in phases. Let us see how it happened.

Athens in peacetime was a city where one could die of boredom. The slaves did all the work and those who were fortunate enough to be citizens hardly knew how to pass the time. It must have been a problem just getting through the day. Given this situation, it is easy enough to understand the popularity of courtroom dramas: imagine having nothing but Perry Mason on television.

Before the arrival of Pericles, professional pleaders were not allowed in Greek courts. The citizen, whatever his role, plaintiff or defendant, had to appear in person and present his own case: it was just bad luck if he did not happen to be a good speaker.

The jury, or *Heliaia*,[1] was made up of ordinary citizens; they were men of impeccable character, but not being trained lawyers they were often swayed by the cleverness of the speaker rather than the validity of the argument, so the cunning nearly always got away with it at the expense of the inarticulate.

The first to take advantage of the plight of country-dwellers involved with the law was the Athenian Antiphon. As a political exile, Antiphon had taken up residence in Corinth where, to survive, he had opened a 'shop of consolation', or a studio where, he claimed, any

[1] See J. Burckhardt, *op. cit.*, p. 82.

kind of mental suffering could be cured by the simple power of speech. After several years as a professional consoler, he had the idea of writing speeches for anybody who had to appear in court. And so efficacious were the texts he dreamt up that he soon became known all over Attica as 'the concocter of discourses'.[2] Included in the account he presented to his clients was the fee for one lesson in oratory during which he expected the speech to be learnt by heart because, since his clientele was largely illiterate, there was no other way he could deliver the goods.

Antiphon and others like him were called *logographoi*; their business was to write, on demand, political speeches, funeral orations and forensic arguments for use in murder trials. Some *logographoi*, by passing themselves off as relatives of the accused, even managed to appear as defence witnesses for a client. Within a few years they had made themselves sufficiently indispensable to be accorded legal recognition by the tribunals. Those who practised the profession of *rhetor*, or paid orator, were the Sophists: their speciality was the art of public speaking.

To begin with, the word 'Sophist' had no negative connotations at all, quite the contrary: the root of the word, *sophia*, means 'wisdom', and 'to be a Sophist' meant 'to have a profound knowledge in some special field'. (The modern technical term would be 'to have the know-how'.) Later, however, the philosophers and intellectuals in general, shocked at the practice of trading intellect for money, ganged up against them and did everything possible to give them a bad name. Xenophon, in the *Memorabilia*,[3] says: 'There are some men called Sophists who prostitute themselves and sell their own knowledge in exchange for money to all who ask. They speak to deceive and write for gain and nobody is the better for it.' In several of the dialogues, Plato, not to be outdone, engineered their humiliation at the hands of a Socrates more sophistic than themselves.

The bad blood between Sophists and philosophers was aggravated by a difference in professional set-up. The 'traditional' philosophers were usually connected with a school having its own rules and

---

[2]See *I Presocratici, cit.*, vol. II, p. 982.
[3]Xenophon, *Memorabilia* I 1, 11.

doctrines, whereas the Sophists worked the market as free-lance professionals and saw no need to espouse any particular ideology. This is a substantial difference when you remember that the Greek schools of philosophy were rather like brotherhoods where the students, as well as receiving instruction, shared a common faith; from their point of view, therefore, the Sophists were men without scruples and without ideals. It never occurred to them that the Sophists might believe in one simple truth, that of the non-existence of Truth itself.

In spite of being boycotted by the intelligentsia, the Sophists became ever more popular, a few even achieving the kind of celebrity usually reserved for Olympic champions. Each had his own style of oratory or some distinguishing quality that marked him out from the rest. Hippias of Elis, for example, wore only clothes and other articles he had made himself;[4] even his sandals and the engraved ring on his finger were all his own work; and besides this, his memory was prodigious despite his eighty years: it was said that he could repeat fifty names, in the right order, after hearing them only once.[5] Isocrates had more than a hundred students each of whom paid a fee of one hundred drachmas – unless he was Athenian, in which case the course was free.[6] Gorgias of Leontini was capable of improvising an oration on any subject that was proposed to him.[7] Antiphon of Rhamnus would write four speeches for the same trial, one for and one against the prosecution, one for and one against the defence.[8] Prodicus of Ceos would wake up an audience that showed signs of dropping off by suddenly shouting at them: 'Attention! Attention! I am about to tell you something that will cost you fifty drachmas!'[9] Protagoras of Abdera, speaking to a poet who had insulted him in the street, said: 'I much prefer listening to your insults than to your poetry.'[10] Lysias, possibly the most stylish orator of them all, was noted for the extreme simplicity of his language. This is how he

[4]Plato, *Hippias Minor* 368b.

[5]Philostratus, *Lives of the Sophists* I 11, 1.

[6]See *Vitarum scriptores Graeci minores*, ed. A. Westermann, Brunswick 1845, pp. 254–5.

[7]Philostratus, *Lives of the Sophists* I, 1, 8.

[8]See Cantarella, *La letteratura greca classica*, Florence 1967, p. 444.

[9]Aristotle, *Rhetoric* III 14 1415b 12.

[10]See *I Presocratici, cit.*, vol. II, p. 888.

concludes his oration *Against Eratosthenes*: 'I have come to the end of the accusation. You have heard, you have seen, and the decision now rests with you. Pronounce your verdict.'[11] The subtle Hypereides put his faith in the emotional susceptibility of the jury. His speech for the defence of Euxenippus ends with the words: 'I have helped you as much as I could. All that remains is for you to appeal to the judges, call your friends and summon your children.'[12] The politician Cleon used to stride up and down while speaking, throwing back his robe and slapping his thigh.[13]

The form of oratory that gave the Sophists the greatest delight was *epideitic*, an art whose sole purpose was to show off the eloquence of the speaker. Actual contests of epideitic rhetoric were held in Athens; the Sophists would match themselves against each other, there were competitive examinations for aspiring rhetors and on one occasion a competition to find the best funeral elegy (fans may like to know that the compulsory theme on this occasion was a certain Mausolus).[14] Among the orations that have left their mark on history we might mention Lucan's *In Praise of a Fly* and, above all, Gorgias of Leontini's *Encomium on Helen*. Here the Sophist argues that the poor lady could in no way be blamed for what happened between the Greeks and the Trojans. There are three possible hypotheses, says Gorgias: Troy's destiny had been preordained by the Fates and the Gods, in which case they were responsible; or she was violently abducted, in which case she was as much the victim of Paris's action as anybody else; or she was persuaded by what he said to her, and 'in this case, O Athenians, be assured that there is nothing in the world so much to be feared as the word: the word is a sovereign power, because although it is physically tiny and completely invisible, it is the agent by which the most divine works are brought to fulfilment.'[15]

One form of epideictic rhetoric was *antilogic*, the 'two-sided argument'. The Sophist would first defend a proposition and then, using equally irrefutable arguments, prove the exact opposite. There is a

[11]Lysias XIV 40.
[12]Pliny, *Epistulae* II 11.
[13]Plutarch, *Life of Nicias* 8.
[14]J. Burckhardt, *op. cit.*, p. 296.
[15]Gorgias, *Encomium on Helen* 11, 8.

story that one of the masters of this art went to Rome to demonstrate his skill. When he came to the end of the first part of his demonstration he was greeted with loud applause, but when he began to argue the counter-proposition he was set upon and most earnestly thrashed. The Romans were a simple people of few words: some of the refinements of Greek culture were completely beyond them.

XXIII
Protagoras

rotagoras, nicknamed 'Reasoning',[1] was the son of Artemon or Meandrius and was born in Abdera around 480 BC.[2]

His family was poor so he did what he could to earn a living by working as a porter for local traders. One day Democritus saw him at work and was immediately struck by the ingenious way the young man had organized a load of wood on his mule. 'Someone who can do that,' he thought, 'must have a natural predisposition for philosophical reasoning' – and without more ado offered him a place in his school.[3]

The youth very soon became an able speaker. After a spell in his native city, where he was engaged to give public readings, we next hear of him as a teacher of rhetoric in Athens. Philostratus says that he was the first to charge a fee of one hundred minas for a course in oratory and 'to introduce this custom among the Greeks, which was welcomed on the grounds that everyone takes more seriously something for which they have paid than something that is free.'[4]

Protagoras must have been extremely expensive. His pupil Euathlus, horrified at being asked for a thousand dinars at the end of his course, tried to avoid payment, suggesting that the fee should only become due after he had scored his first success in court. Protagoras was unmoved. He said: 'Dear Euathlus, you've got no choice, because

[1]See *I Presocratici, cit.*, vol. II, p. 877.
[2]Diogenes Laertius, *op. cit.* IX 50.
[3]Diogenes Laertius, *op. cit.* IX 53.
[4]Philostratus, *Lives of the Sophists*, I 3, 4.

I shall immediately bring charges against you. If you lose, you will have to pay because you have lost, if you win, you will have to pay because you have won.'[5]

Such a cantankerous character was bound to be unpopular in Athens, and he was. It is quite likely, however, that the root cause of this dislike was jealousy of the substantial fortune he had amassed in such a short time. The poet and playwright Euopolis describes him as 'a wicked fraud-monger dealing in celestial things',[6] and Plato, in one of the dialogues, makes Socrates say: 'I know of a man, Protagoras, who earned more money from his profession than an outstandingly fine craftsman like Phidias and ten other sculptors put together'.[7]

He exercised his profession for forty years and wrote a dozen books including two anthologies and an essay on religious sentiment called *On the Gods* of which he himself give a public reading at the house of Euripides.[8]

When he was seventy, Fortune turned against him. The Athenians put him on trial for having written the following words: 'As to the Gods, I have no means of knowing either that they exist or that they do not exist. For many are the obstacles that impede knowledge, both the obscurity of the question and the shortness of human life.'[9] His accuser was Pythodorus, one of the Four Hundred who had overthrown the democratic government in Athens.[10] Protagoras fled from Greece to escape the draught of hemlock and was on his way to Sicily, pursued by the triremes of Athens, when the ship in which he was sailing sank off the Sicilian coast.[11] The Athenians burnt his books in the market-place after organizing a house-to-house search for every copy in circulation.[12] The poet Timon of Phlius dedicated the following lines to him:

To the first of all the Sophists, before and after,/he of the beautiful voice, of sharp and versatile skill: Protagoras./ They wished to reduce his works to

[5]Quintilian, *Institutiones oratoriae* III 1, 12.
[6]Eustathius, *Commentary on the Odyssey* (1546), 53.
[7]Plato, *Meno*, 91 D.
[8]Diogenes Laertius, *op. cit.* IX 54.
[9]Diogenes Laertius, *op. cit.* IX 52.
[10]Aristotle, fr. 67 Rose.
[11]Philostratus, *Lives of the Sophists* I 10, 3.
[12]Diogenes Laertius, *op. cit.* IX 52.

ashes, for/ he wrote that he did not know or understand/ the Gods, who and what they are,/ having the greatest care for impartiality./ It profited him not, and he sought to flee to avoid/ drinking the bitter draught of Socrates and descending into Hades.[13]

Protagoras' philosophy is summed up in the following phrase:

Man is the measure of all things, of things that are that they are, and of things that are not that they are not.[14]

Philosophers are divided in their interpretation of this. They ask: Who is the man here to whom Protagoras is referring? Is it just any man, any Tom, Dick or Harry? Or is it Man in general, Man with a capital M representing the average opinion of the whole category of men? We have to be precise on this point because it governs our judgement of the Philosopher.

My personal view is that the first suggestion is right. The man Protagoras is speaking about is me, Luciano De Crescenzo, son of Eugenio De Crescenzo and Giulia née Panetta, with all the qualities, negative and positive, pertaining to me. What I know is not an objective reality which is the same for everyone, but one that only assumes a particular significance the moment 'I' perceive it, and naturally this significance changes from moment to moment as my own opinions fluctuate.

The relativism expressed in Protagoras' phrase applies both to the field of knowledge and to that of ethics.

Seeing that the same orangeade can seem sweet to a man in perfect health and sour to one who is ill, the Sophist asks: 'Is this orangeade sweet or sour?' It is both, for the very reason that two people have tasted it. Neither opinion is *truer* than the other; all we can say is that the opinion of the healthy man is *preferable* to the opinion of the sick man on the grounds that a healthy condition is more frequent than an unhealthy one. The conclusion, then, is that the truth about anything varies from person to person, and for each individual from one moment to the next.

There is general agreement up to this point; the problems begin

[13]See *I Prestocratici, cit.,* vol. II, p. 881.
[14]Diogenes Laertius, *op. cit.* IX 51.

the moment we get entangled in the thornbush of a common ethic. Do Good and Evil exist as objective realities, or is it up to us to decide for ourselves what is Good and what is Evil? That is the question.

Until the Sophists arrived on the scene, the views of ancient peoples had been reasonably cut and dried. Actions were judged black or white and there was an end to it. At the time, Zoroastrianism was taking the Near East by storm and this was a religion which divided the world into two camps, the Good and the Evil, allowing nothing in between. Perhaps the greatest merit of the Sophists lies precisely in their invention of the Grey Zone as an intermediate stage between the extremes, and in their having sown the seed of doubt that is tantamount to an invitation to look always, in every instance, at the other side of the coin. Protagoras can be seen as the father of Scepticism and the grandfather of Popper.

Some people might object that 'to act the Sophist' is rather too convenient. For example, it allows me to define theft, murder and lying as the Good, and then to do anything I like without violating my personal code of morals. 'OK,' says Protagoras, 'if you can do that, go ahead.' But in point of fact, it is not that easy to convince one's own conscience that stealing and killing are identifiable with the Good. And this is where we have to decide how far Protagoras' relativism is conditioned by ordinary morality. We agree that we are the judges, but we cannot deny that our judgement is influenced by the ethical norm.

To those who support the view that Protagoras was referring to Man with a capital M, the Philosopher might have said that the Good was identical with the Good of Man in general and therefore with the collective Good. He may have uttered a similar phrase but we can be sure that he did not believe it. It was not the way his mind worked. Who knows, perhaps when he was facing his judges, he might have said something of the kind for fear of Critias (an ex-Sophist who became one of the Thirty Tyrants and, as such, a ferocious persecutor of his ex-colleagues), but as he walked away afterwards, he would have muttered to himself, like Galileo, 'Man in general does not exist!'

We, on the other hand, encouraged by his slogan, can interpret it how we like, convinced that we are indeed the measure of all things, of those that are and of those that are not. And if we want proof of this, we only have to listen to two fans of opposing teams each giving his own account of a football derby. In perfectly good faith, each will report on 'his' match, ignoring the mistakes, the wrong decisions and any bad luck claimed by the other, and this for the simple reason that he has not 'wanted to see' anything to the detriment of his own side. So what is Truth? 'All and nothing', as Pirandello said. Reality is what we invent for ourselves as we go along. If we do not enjoy our work, we read the horoscope and believe that something better is around the corner. If a girlfriend deserts us, we tell ourselves that she must have been called abroad on business. If the Italian national debt is in the region of 100,000 billion, we ignore the fact and continue to live as before, strong in the knowledge that the economic crisis is nothing new and that it has never caused us any personal inconvenience.

XXIV
Gorgias of Leontini

orn between 480 and 475 BC, Gorgias was a native of
Leontini (or Lentini, as we know it today) in Sicily. We
know nothing about the first fifty years of his life except
that his father's name was Carmantidas and that his brother, Her-
odicus, was a physician.[1] It is assumed that he knew and was taught by
Empedocles. The first real information we have about him comes
from Diodorus[2] and refers to a deputation sent from Leontini to
Athens in 427 to ask for military help against the power of Syracuse.
Gorgias led the mission.

The Sophist presented himself in the Athenian *agora* robed in
purple from head to foot[3] and accompanied by a fellow orator from
Leontini, one Tisias. Alternating on the dais, the two ambassadors
excited great admiration. Never before had the Athenians experienced oratory like this![4] According to Philostratus,[5] Gorgias demonstrated 'oratorical drive, innovatory audacity, inspired gestures,
sublime tone, the ability to pause effectively and resume dramatically,
poetic expression and tasteful decoration'. A pity tape recorders
weren't around at the time: we should then have known what the devil
Suidas meant by describing Gorgias as 'inventor of the rhetorical use

Pausanius, VI 17, 7.
Diodorus Siculus, XII 53, 1.
Aelian, *Various History* XII 32.
Diodorus Siculus, XII 53, 3.
Philostratus, *Lives of the Sophists* I 9, 2.

of tropes, hypallage, catachresis, hyperbaton, anadiplosis, epanadiplosis and parisa'.[6]

Gorgias soon became a star, making appearances in the theatres and shouting to the people in the stalls: 'Give me a theme!'[7] Isocrates maintains that he earned more than all the other Sophists;[8] he became so rich that he presented the Delphic oracle with a life-size golden statue of himself as a thank offering to Apollo.[9] He was invited to Thessaly by the tyrant Jason and ever afterwards the Thessalians referred to the art of rhetoric as 'The art of Gorgias'.[10]

It appears that he married rather late in life but had problems with his wife on account of an extra-marital involvement.[11] A certain Melanthius, in fact, pokes fun at him, saying: 'This man gives advice about domestic harmony but has been unable to achieve agreement between himself, his wife and his maidservant, and they are only three.'

Gorgias' most important work is his book *On Nature or the Non-Existent*, but his speeches, including the *Encomium on Helen* which we have already mentioned, the *Defence of Palamedes*, and the *Pythian, Olympic* and *Funeral* orations, are just as famous.

He lived to be 108 and when asked how he managed to reach such a great age he replied: 'By renouncing pleasure'. He might have lived even longer had he not, as some maintain, brought about his own end by refusing food.[12] When the fatal moment came, the cue for a dramatic exit line was too good to miss: 'Behold how sleep now begins to deliver me into her sister's arms.'[13]

One day a passing swallow scored a direct hit on Gorgias' head; the Sophist glanced up, gave the bird a very severe look and exclaimed reproachfully: 'Shame on you, Philomela!'[14] This anecdote survives

[6]Cf. *I Presocratici, cit.*, vol. II, pp. 905–6.
[7]Cicero, *De inventione* V 2.
[8]Isocrates, XV 155ff.
[9]Pliny, *Natural History* XXXIII 83.
[10]Philostratus, *Epistola* 73.
[11]Plutarch, *Advice to the Married* 43; 144 B-C.
[12]Lucan, *Longevity* 23.
[13]Aelian, *Various History* II 35.
[14]Philomela was seduced by Tereus, the husband of her sister, Procne. To

thanks to Aristotle,[16] who used it as an example of the incorrect use of metaphor. Gorgias of Leontini, says the Fount of All Wisdom, 'makes two errors here: the first in blaspheming the name of the dead (and the comic and the tragic must never be combined), and the second in feigning to ignore the fact that it was not Tereus' wife who was caught short out of doors but only a poor swallow.' Needless to say, Aristotle had no sense of humour and was, moreover, no friend of the Sophists. Not only did he criticize Gorgias over the swallow episode, but even cast doubt on his very existence as a philosopher. In those days, as I said before and will now repeat, to get on the wrong side of Plato or Aristotle, the virtual godfathers of Greek philosophy, meant having one's name struck off the register of philosophers. And their influence, far from decreasing over the years, has in fact conditioned opinion ever since. Even today one can read comments like: 'The nihilism of Gorgias should form no part of the history of philosophy,' and 'his ironic discourse on nature has no place except in the history of rhetoric'.[17]

But we, in our small way, shall reinstate the philosophical content in Gorgias' work even while disagreeing with its moral aspect. Perhaps it is just his extraordinary rhetorical ability that throws the historians; most of them in fact tended to regard Gorgias as nothing but an exceptional orator and his celebrated speeches as nothing but rhetorical virtuosity. Yet the celebrated *Apologias* for Helen and Palamedes themselves yield genuine insight into Gorgias' philosophy. In these speeches the Sophist puts all the emphasis on form at the expense of content; he is not interested in the actions of the faithless wife or the man who betrayed Ulysses but offloads all responsibility on to the word as a means of persuasion.

'Nothing exists; if anything does exist, it is unknowable; and granting it even to exist and to be knowable by any one man, it could never be communicated to any others.'[17] These are the opening words of his book *On Nature or the Non-Existent*.

---

prevent his wife hearing about this Tereus tried to kill the unfortunate girl, but she was saved at the last minute by being transformed into a nightingale.

[15] Aristotle, *Rhetoric* III 3, 1406b 14.

[16] H. Gomperz, *Sophistik und Rhetorik,* Leipzig 1912, p. 35.

[17] Sextus Empiricus, *Adversus Mathematicos* VII 65.

This premise allows Gorgias to deny reality more completely than Parmenides, Zeno or Melissus. They at least admitted the existence of the One; Gorgias even denies that. Anyone who professes any faith at all is bound to take exception to such a statement; it is tantamount to Gorgias having said: 'My dear sirs, with all due respect, Truth does not exist, or, if you prefer, is not within our reach, which is, for all practical purposes, the same thing. All you can cling to is *the correlation of the logos*, or the possibility of exercising power through word and thought.'

Two points to ponder with regard to this character:

1 It would be hard to imagine a more tedious life than that of Gorgias: 108 years of believing in nothing and renouncing pleasure.

2 Even conceding the impossibility of knowing the Truth, one can still ask which is more important, that Truth exists or that one can grasp it?

In my opinion, *Truth exists, because if it did not exist, the fact of its non-existence would exist to an even lesser degree.* The only way to arrive logically at a proof of the existence of Truth (or God) is by a positive negative:

'Can you say that you are sure that God exists?'

'No.'

'Can you say that you are sure that God does not exist?'

'No, to be honest.'

'Then you admit that something exists that you do not know.'

'Yes.'

'Be so kind, then, as to call this thing that exists without your knowing it "God".'

'And if I prefer to call it simply "that which I do not know"?'

'It makes no difference, the meaning's the same.'

This reminds me of a famous story by Borges called *The Library of Babel*.[18] The writer imagines himself in an enormous building rather like a beehive laid out with hexagonal galleries every one of which is lined with books. In the middle of each gallery is an enormous ventilation shaft affording a glimpse, upwards and downwards, of an infinite succession of other hexagonal halls, all filled with books; and

[18]J. L. Borges, *Fictions*, pp. 72ff (London, 1985, translated by Anthony Kerrigan).

even if one passes into another gallery, one finds oneself in another vertical system identical to the first: a nightmarish conception.

The books in the Library of Babel are of uniform length, 410 pages and all incomprehensible: hrydghbdrskh ... one reads in a volume picked at random. After a lot of thought, an old man discovers that the books contain no more and no less than every possible combination of the letters of the alphabet; the library must therefore contain an enormous number of books.

Given the random combinations, every now and then a phrase will occur in some book that makes a kind of sense, like: *O time thy pyramids*. But when it becomes known that this 'Universal Library' contains all the possible books, someone suggests that it must also contain *The Book of Books*, the volume that divulges the Secret of Life itself. From that point the search becomes frenzied, groups of men throwing themselves upon the volumes as if possessed, snatching at them blindly only to throw them down again as soon as they ascertain that the text is incomprehensible. The only one not to move is Borges himself: satisfied with the knowledge that the Book is there somewhere, he concludes: *'May Heaven exist, though my place be in Hell. Let me be outraged and annihilated, but may Thy enormous Library be justified, for one instant, in one being.'*

XXV
Avvocato Tanucci

Armà datte curaggie, tenimme 'a causa 'mmano.
'A parte ha miso a Porzio, mammà mette a Marciano.

he words of a Neapolitan mother, shouted out, according to a poem by Rocco Galdieri,[1] as she runs behind the prison van. 'Armando, don't you worry, we've got the case in hand. The other side's got Porzio, but mother's got Marciano.' Giovanni Porzio and Gennaro Marciano were the two outstanding forensic lawyers in Naples during the first half of this century. In those days criminal trials aroused extraordinary enthusiasm, the common folk attending proceedings in the Courts of Assize as regularly as the Italian public today watches *Dallas* and *Dynasty*. As soon as someone said 'Porzio's speaking!' everyone listened with bated breath.

When the trial of the 'Bella Veneziana' was under way, the Neapolitan public was behind her to a man. The case was a classic crime of passion: Antonietta Catullo, an unmarried mother, had killed her seducer in Villa Comunale. Her defending counsel, Alfredo Catapano, ended his speech to the jury with the words: 'Set her free in the name of every woman who has been subjected to violence, deceit and betrayal; every woman who, out of her need for love, has taken false promises at their face value, every woman exposed to evil, poverty and deprivation who has found the strength to rise again, to live and

[1]Rocco Galdieri, *Mamme napulitane*, in a collection of poetry published by Bideri, Naples 1953.

rehabilitate herself through the love and protection of a child.'
The 'Venetian Beauty' was acquitted and Naples went wild with
joy. Hundreds of women carried Avvocato Catapano shoulder
high, singing:

> *Tu hai difeso 'a causa,*
> *Alfredo Catapano,*
> *e mò 'a gente 'e mane*
> *sbatteno pe' ttè.*[2]

The courts of justice in Naples are housed in an ancient castle,
the notorious Castel Capuano, built around the year 1000 by
William II. Originally a fortress, it became successively a court, a
private residence and finally a prison and law courts under the
Spanish viceroy Don Pedro da Toledo.

Apart from the cars, I doubt if the precincts of the old castle
have changed very much since the days of the Spanish viceroys.
The gloomy pile still dominates the surrounding area. The narrow streets and the bars swarm with lawyers, street traders,
loafers, prisoners on parole, relatives awaiting the arrival of a
detainee, pickpockets on the look-out for likely victims. Standing half-way between the mean streets of the Duchesca, where
the goods on offer are too cheap even to qualify as bargains, and
the nearby Porta Capuana, drowned by the noise of car horns,
the courts swallow and spew out an endless, multicoloured
stream of people who are by now resigned to treating the Law as
the equivalent of any meteorological disturbance.

Not all the lawyers who throng the spacious forecourt of
Castel Capuano are forensic giants. Among them one can, more
or less, distinguish five separate categories: star practitioners,
run-of-the-mill practitioners, *paglietta* (see below), *strascinaf-*
acenne (ditto) and juniors.

The stars are those who leave their mark on legal history:
Nicola Amore, Enrico Pessina and Leopoldo Tarantini of the

[2]'You defended her, Alfredo Catapano, and now the people applaud
you.'

nineteenth century, Gennaro Marciano, Giovanni Porzio, Enrico De Nicola and Alfredo De Marsico of the twentieth are the first names that spring to mind. Each had a personality and a style of oratory that distinguished him from the others: passionate in the case of Marciano, lyrical in that of De Marsico, cold and clear in De Nicola's.

On one occasion a great criminal lawyer, Avvocato Gaetano Manfredi, concluded his speech to the jury maybe rather over-emphatically: 'They are saying in the streets that this case is lost. Very well, so it may be; but if I fall it will be like a wounded eagle with wing outspread and eye fixed upon the sun.' His opposing counsel, Carlo Fiorante, nicknamed 'the caustic', replied wither-ingly: 'All that matters to us is that you fall; as for the rest, feel free to choose any position that appeals to you.'

The *strascinafacenne*, sometimes qualified, sometimes not, are legal odd-jobbers. They do everything: legal form-filling, passports, renewals of certificates and licences, traffic viola-tions, et cetera, et cetera. The name (derived from *strascicare*, to drag, to draw out, and *faccenda*, affair, business) is applied to them because as soon as they get their hands on a good custo-mer they 'drag out the business' as long as possible with the object of obtaining a succession of small emoluments.

The juniors are usually ageing assistants to leading counsel with several decades of legal experience under their belt. Even if not fully qualified, their knowledge of law is often far more comprehensive than that of their leaders.

The *paglietta* is part of the history of Naples and first appeared on the judicial scene of Naples in the seventeenth century. Camillo Gurgo gives us the following description:[3] 'Pot-bellied, comical, something between a priest and a knight, he wore silken knee-breeches, big shoes ornamented with large shiny metal buckles, a fitted over-garment popularly called *sar-aca*, neck-bands of the faded blue colour actually known as *paglietta*, an enormous straw hat with black silk ribbons and a sword at his side.'

[3]Camillo Gurgo, *Castel Capuano e i paglietta*, Naples 1929.

By the eighteenth century, the *paglietta*, or Neapolitan Sophist in the pejorative sense of the word, had changed somewhat; he had become tall and thin and his style of dress had deteriorated. Cerlone, a contemporary playwright, lampooned him by creating the character of Don Fastidio de' Fastidiis, a pettifogging, blustering ditherer. Benedetto Croce, on behalf of the Neapolitan legal profession and, perhaps, the Greek Sophists, objected to this and was at pains to point out that de' Fastidiis is more a caricature of a simple-minded boor than a *paglietta* because despite the latter's shortcomings in the field of professional ethics, the one thing he positively could not be accused of was simple-mindedness. But Don Fastidio de' Fastidiis is a bumbler pure and simple. In one of the plays he is made to say to a noblewoman whom he wishes to compliment on her merits: 'Oh my dear *meretrice!*' – meaning prostitute.

The *paglietta* is as active in the courts today as he ever was. He is probably one of those characters that endure down the ages like the Man in the Iron Mask. Plautus sketched him in the following words: *Os habet linguam, perfidiam, malitiam, atque audaciam, confidentiam, confirmitatem, fraudolentiam.* (His mouth has tongue, perfidy, mischief, as well as brazenness, conceit, obstinacy, cunning.)

Two thousand years later, Maddalari maintained that 'the *paglietta* is unique in Naples in not suffering from the disease of Ideals; in this he is even superior to the janitors who are, let's be honest, practical and down-to-earth.'

I made the acquaintance of one of them. His name is Annibale Tanucci. His motto is: 'Justice is like a tight shoe: it requires a shoe-horn.'

To give you an idea of the man, I quote one of his closing speeches.

Your honours, members of the jury, we are here to defend the good character of Signor Alessandro Esposito, otherwise called *'a Rinascente*, against the imputation of fraud and misappropriation of a protected trade mark.

We intend to prove that as no fraud was involved there is no case to answer with regard to the first charge, and that my client's activities, in respect of misappropriation of a trade mark, do not, in fact, constitute a breach of the law.

Bearing that in mind, let us now proceed to the facts of the case:

On Sunday 27 March, Palm Sunday, a fine sunny morning such as one might reasonably expect to inspire nothing but goodwill among men, an officer of the urban constabulary, Michele Abbondanza, imposed the penalty of a fine upon my client Alessandro Esposito for selling assorted bags and handbags without a licence upon the pavement in front of the church of Santa Caterina in Chiaia. On the following day, a search carried out by Customs and Excise officers at a ground-floor dwelling situated at number 25, Vico Sergente Maggiore, the residence of my client, revealed the existence of a modest production unit for the manufacture of the above-mentioned bags and handbags, manned exclusively by members of the Esposito family, and of twenty-eight watches in perfect working order, being imitations of the following makes: Rolex, Cartier, Porsche and Piaget.

To arrive at the crux of the case against my client, I must make it quite clear that the plastic material, bought in by Esposito for assembling the bags but not manufactured by him, was overprinted, both horizontally and vertically, by a series of the letters 'L' and 'V', intertwined to form monograms and separated by a design of small flowers. These letters are reputed to be the initials of a certain Louis Vuitton, a citizen of the French Republic, not present in this courtroom and whom I do not have the pleasure of knowing.

In case the information of the honourable members of the jury should not be entirely up to date in respect of the price of goods produced by the company of Louis Vuitton of Paris, I will take the liberty of informing them that a medium-sized handbag made of best-quality French plastic retails at around 400,000 lire, whereas the Italian replica produced by my client costs only 25,000 lire and, in some instances, when the day's takings have been unsatisfactory, even 20,000. Please to remark

one fundamental detail: above all the goods was displayed a
large placard bearing the words:

AUTHENTIC LOUIS VUITTON HANDBAGS
IMITATED TO PERFECTION.

Now, one asks, is Alessandro Esposito guilty of fraud? But what
does the term 'fraud' imply? Let's refer to the statute book. Let's
see ... Article number 640 ... 'Whoever shall by the use of
artifice or deception mislead another and by so doing accrue to
himself dishonest profit shall, upon the complaint of the offended party being upheld, be liable to imprisonment for a minimum of three months and a maximum of three years and to a
fine not less than 40,000 lire and not greater than 400,000.' From
this we deduce that the charge of fraud in the first place ineluc-
tably presupposes an offended party who has been defrauded.
So who is this offended party? The passing customer? Indeed
not, learned members of the tribunal, because there are two
possibilities: either the passing customer had read the placard
in its entirety, in which case he or she was well aware of the fact
that the goods were mere imitations, or, for whatever reason, he
or she had only read the words AUTHENTIC LOUIS VUITTON HAND-
BAGS, in which case the customer is himself or herself guilty of
deception in expecting to acquire, for only 20,000 lire, an article
having a retail value of nearly half a million! And, at the end of
the day, where is the dishonest profit? The nine or ten thousand
lire per handbag that Esposito took home to his waiting family of
workers? No, your honours: the defence firmly maintains that,
as no one has been defrauded, no fraud has been perpetrated.

And now let's turn to the second charge: misappropriation of
a protected trade mark. The old masters such as Giotto,
Cimabue and Masaccio were not in the habit of signing their
masterpieces, rightly maintaining that a work of art should be
appreciated for its intrinsic qualities and not because it happens
to bear the signature of Smith or Jones. The insistence upon
signatures can, in fact, be regarded as a perversion of the con-
sumer society of our times. Today, human idiocy – I apologize
for the coarseness of the term – has reached the point where

people are prepared to buy anything provided it bears the right label.

Back in the Fifties, the painter Piero Manzoni carried out a deliberately provocative experiment: he succeeded in marketing his own faeces, having sealed them (we hope) hermetically in a tin and labelled them 'artist's excrement'. Now, Monsieur Louis Vuitton of Paris was working on precisely the same principle, when, one fine day, he thought to himself: 'I shall make thousands of plastic handbags, write my initials upon them and market them at ten times their real value. Then we'll see how many idiots will be duped into buying them.' I mention Vuitton, but the same argument applies naturally to all the other companies who market labels: Gucci, Fendi, Armani, Rolex, et cetera et cetera. There are no limits any longer: even when sitting on the toilet one can derive satisfaction from being surrounded with tiles signed by Valentino!

Someone might raise the following objection: 'Louis Vuitton forces nobody to buy his handbags. Why does your client, instead of making free with other people's labels, not launch his own product on the market?' Quite so. But can you imagine one lady saying to another: 'I bought an Esposito yesterday, you should just see how smart it is!'

Having come this far, I now find myself wondering: is there any law which limits the profits of the individual? Yes, there is, but it is the law of supply and demand. By raising the retail price of its merchandise above a certain limit, a company will find itself forced under by the competition. But if this company should brainwash its customers by convincing them that the product is of exceptionally high quality when the basic material is synthetic, what then? This is the crunch, my dear Monsieur Vuitton! Article 603: crimes of coercion. 'Any person imposing his will upon another in such a way as to reduce the other to a state of complete subjugation shall be liable to a term of imprisonment ranging from three years to fifteen years.' Now it is my opinion that an individual who has deliberately set out to convince thousands of people that a plastic bag, even when covered in monograms, is of better quality than a similar article in real leather, and has succeeded in so doing, has reduced his customers to a state of complete subjugation, and therefore, in the light of this reasoning, I accuse Monsieur Louis Vuitton of Paris of the crime of coercion. I also accuse the dealers in labels and monograms, the pedlars of thin air, be they Italian or otherwise, of having subjugated and coerced our wives and children. I accuse the fashion magazines such as *Gioia* and *Annabella* of disseminating propaganda on behalf of the false idols of a new fetishism. I accuse the mass media, the advertisers, the dealers and all their accomplices of illicit profiteering. Members of the jury, you hold the scales of justice in your hands. On one side of the balance you see Louis Vuitton, Big International Swindler; on the other Alessandro Esposito, small Neapolitan rogue caught red handed trying to sneak a morsel of bread from the table of the mighty guzzler!

Bibliographical Note

The problem of bibliographies, for a book in translation, is a thorny one. All the primary sources are, of course, equally available in both languages; the only problem here is that of some divergence of detail between English and Italian versions which led, in this case, to the translator occasionally having to act as umpire and give the point sometimes to one side and sometimes to the other. The result was light editing which, if it does not pass unremarked, I hope will be forgiven. Some of the major secondary sources, such as the elegant and dependable *History of Greek Culture* by Jacob Burckhardt, are happily available in English, and for Bertrand Russell's *History of Western Philosophy* one had the luxury of reverting to the original. Other commentaries cited by the author, however, exist only in Italian. Chief among these is *I Presocratici*, edited by Giannantoni (Bari, 1975), to which the author frequently refers his Italian readers. This poses a problem. To include these references would be unhelpful for the majority of English-speaking readers, while to exclude them leaves a gap. The solution was to find an alternative whenever possible. There are many works in English that will further enlighten the reader whose curiosity about Greek thought has been stimulated by the present volume, but possibly none better than John Burnet's *Early Greek Philosophy*. Originally published in 1892, its scholarship remains unimpeachable. The third edition (1920) was an invaluable aid in the preparation of this translation and the translator is more than happy to acknowledge the debt and to repay it, at least partially, by a wholehearted recommendation.

For a colourful, lively and totally enchanting account of Greek life and history during the same period the reader is unhesitatingly referred to H. D. F. Kitto's *The Greeks*.

Bibliography

Selected primary sources:

Aristotle, *Ethics*, translated by H. Rackham (London and Massachusetts 1926, revised edition 1934)

Aristotle, *Metaphysics*, edited and translated by John Warrington (London 1956)

Diogenes Laertius, *Lives of Eminent Philosophers* translated by R. D. Hicks (Harvard 1925)

Herodotus *The Histories*, translated by Aubrey de Sèlincourt (London 1954)

Plato, *The Dialogues*, various translators and dates, edited by Betty Radice (London)

Plutarch's *Lives*, edited and translated by Bernadotte Perrin (Loeb/Heinemann, 1916)

Thucydides, *The Peloponnesian Wars* translated by C. Foster Smith

Collected sayings of the Pre-Socratic Philosophers:

Diels-Kranz: *Die Fragmente der Vorsokratiker* by Hermann Diels edited by Walther Kranz, 5th edition (Berlin 1934)

Note: No English translation.

Commentaries on the Philosophers and on Greek History:

Burckhardt, Jakob, *History of Greek Culture* translated by Palmer Hilty (London 1963)

Burnet, John, *Early Greek Philosophy* (3rd edition London 1920)

Kitto, H. D. F., *The Greeks* (London 1951)

Russell, Bertrand, *History of Western Philosophy* (2nd edition London 1961)

Index

Note: Page references in *bold type* indicate the chief subject of a chapter.